Astral sex – Zen teabags

This book is dedicated to the memory of my brother Tik, who always liked a good laugh.

Astral sex – Zen teabags

Gerry Thompson

with illustrations by Anne Ward and Gerry Thompson

Findhorn Press

British Library Cataloguing-in-Publication Data.
A catalogue record for this book is available from the British Library.

Cover design by WIRE design studio, 34 Sydney Street, Brighton BN1 4EP

Layout and setting by Findhorn Press
Printed and bound by Cromwell Press Ltd, Melksham, England

Published by Findhorn Press, The Park, Findhorn, Forres IV36 0TZ, Moray, Scotland

Postcards of cartoons from this book are available — see page 111

CONTENTS

FOREWORD

Gerry Thompson is one of my favourite cartoonists. I have often groaned in delight at the horribly accurate dissections that he and Anne Ward have perpetrated on our favourite fads and fashions. So I was delighted to find that, in this book, Gerry's satirical sense had found expression in wise and witty words as well as their usual deft drawings.

All the paraphernalia of the New Age is here: from rebirthing to colonic irrigation, chakras to rolfing. *Astral Sex — Zen Teabags* is to the 1990s what *1066 and All That* was to the rest of history. Brought up on Sellers and Yeatman's comic masterpiece, I can promise you that if you liked *1066 and All That*, you'll love this.

Faced with a looming Goliath of ecological dangers and armed only with the home-made catapult of liberal ideals, we need a laugh. We may be devoted to macrobiotics and meditation, but we must have them sent up too: it's unhealthy if you can't laugh at yourself. Affectionate parody is every bit as necessary as coruscating political satire.

So, whether you're a fully paid up necromancer or still struggling with the concept of a mountain bike, this book will tickle your fancy. Read and enjoy. It's a lot more fun than gazing at your navel — and a darn sight easier to do on the train.

Sue Limb

Sue Limb is a writer and broadcaster who is known for Dulcie Domum's 'Bad Housekeeping', the regular column in The Weekend Guardian; *The Wordsmiths of Gorsemere, the book and radio production;* Up the Garden Path, *broadcast on TV and radio; and a number of children's books.*

THE AUTHOR

Gerry Thompson is a writer who also masquerades as a health practitioner. He most recently incarnated in Tipperary, Ireland, but his karma dictated that he be raised in Belfast. He survived a career in architecture and even a profound transformational experience in macrobiotics, before becoming a proper writer.

Gerry is also author of *The Shiatsu Manual,* published internationally in 1994. He is a frequent contributor to a wide range of mainstream and alternative magazines and national newspapers, where his cartoon work also appears. Gerry also writes comedy drama for TV. He is an amateur Buddhist.

Gerry Thompson does live presentations of material such as that contained in this book. He can be contacted at:

34 Sydney Street
Brighton BN1 4EP
UK
Tel 0273 626123 or 563495
Fax 0273 602606

AUTHOR'S NOTE

Offering a guide to any kind of jargon is a daunting task; for jargon, by its very nature, constitutes the use of words which appear to mean something terribly profound, specific and vital, but actually mean very little, if anything at all. In fact, the meaning of much jargon is unknown, though no one can afford to admit that. The main purpose of jargon, then, is not to convey meaning or content, but to identify its user as a knowledgeable, sophisticated and important person.

Explaining so-called 'New Age' jargon is even more challenging, owing to a general lack of agreement at large as to what the New Age is, what it constitutes and includes, or whether it even exists. Even if the New Age does not exist, however, there is no denying that its jargon does exist and, as jargon goes, it is very 'jargony'. New-Age-Speak has the homogeneity that characterises a fully-fledged body of cliché. It is unified by a number of qualities that can easily be mastered by anyone who wishes to present themselves convincingly as an authority in this broad and ill-defined arena. Briefly, the aim seems to be to appear at once arrogant, omniscient, pompous and totally disconnected from reality, and in this way to show how incredibly sensitive, aware, evolved and totally enlightened you really are.

If you follow the guidelines in this book, then, you will surely achieve what appears to be the goal of the true New Age Jargon-monger — not to have a clue what you are talking about. I wish you success.

GT

Abbreviations Used in the Dictionary

a. adjective

n. noun

v. verb

cl. cliché

obs. obsolete (ie currently out of fashion, but not yet revivable)

ps. pseudish

pr. pretentious

ow. overworked

~~**m.**~~ not okay for men to use

erron. erroneous

errat. erratic

erot. erotic

pc. politically correct at time of going to press

Pronunciation

Incorrect pronunciation can give the impression that you are only using a word or phrase in order to enhance your own image, which is probably true but is the last thing you want people to realise. Please pay special attention to the pronunciation guidelines provided.

*Items that occur in the text in **bold italics** have their own entries elsewhere in the book. Where a number of meanings are given, they are listed in order of pretentiousness.*

Affirmations

Things that people repeat *ad nauseam* about what they would like to have happen in their lives, instead of actually doing something about it. Anita de Lujonne's definitive work, *Teach Yourself Affirmation Writing,* shows that affirmations can be created for almost any situation, and gives helpful guidance on structure, syntax, accepted terminology and so on. Ample examples are provided, on all kinds of specialised topics. Affirmations for Constipation, for instance — "Abundant poos flow from me now with Joy and Ease." Or "My Intestines are my Friend" (or should it be 'Friends'?). Other realms of life are equally well served: "There is an infinite supply of energy (substitute 'chocolate biscuits', 'toilet paper', 'condoms', 'marijuana' etc as appropriate) in the universe for me to draw upon right now."

Ms de Lujonne also provides a set of useful pro-forma templates into which you can substitute your own requirements. The classic form used for treating insecurity is a case in point: "I am Safe. Life is Safe. The world is a Safe Place. My job is Safe. My car is Safe. My money is Safe. My pet gerbil is Safe." Another good format: "Every day, in every way, my orgasms are getting better and better and better — and . . . er . . . my girlfriend is having quite a good time too."

To summarise de Lujonne's authoritative guidance, the idea is to be as smug and egocentric as possible, throw in lots of subsidiary words and phrases such as 'abundant', 'magnet', 'right now' and of course the ubiquitous 'I/my/me/myself', plus as many superlatives as possible. Truly great affirmations, however, have to be ambitious, arrogant, pompous, wildly unrealistic and laden with impatience. In this line, de Lujonne finishes with her all-time favourites:

> "Everyone adores me, and I can hardly blame them."
> "I am always in the Right Place, doing the Right Thing with the Right Person."
> "There is no getting away from it, I am Simply Better than everyone else."

TOMORROW I WILL START LIVING IN THE PRESENT

Recent research has shown that almost all adult affirmers displayed an identical profile when they were children at school — low self-esteem, forever in detention, and having to do lines all the time.

See also **Negative Affirmations**

AKASHIC

Name given to the records pertaining to everything that has ever happened, or will ever happen, anywhere, at any time (or that has even been contemplated). Their existence is widely accepted today, but unfortunately no one knows how to consult them. They were probably set up by a Virgo with Aquarius rising. Still, it's good to know they're there.

ALIEN

Anyone from another galaxy who cares more about our planet than we do.

ALLERGIES

See **Intolerance**.

ANGELS

Generic term for a wide variety of species of helpful entities whom some human beings can occasionally see or otherwise directly perceive through the senses. Their main purpose is to help the higher powers to run the universe, and to minimise the damage done to Creation by humans. Some of the more frequently encountered species are listed here.

Archangels: Quite high-up entities who can be recognised by the fact that their wings meet over their heads.

Fairies: A large subspecies which originally specialised in cakes but has since become much more diverse, nowadays tending to meddle in almost anything. The whole angelic host, in fact, at one time was only concerned with cake-making, which was regarded as a very important archetypal activity with enormous potential for creating both good and evil. The residue of this work is still in evidence in human affairs, through such enduring institutions as Angel Cake, Fairy Cakes, Devil's Food Cake and Death by Chocolate.

Leprechauns: Small angels in green tights.

Devas: These ones are fond of opera, and can have a bit of the prima-donna about them. Their favourite hobby is gardening.

Hoovas: Household cleaning spirits.

Ravas: Sprites who have special responsibility for looking after people on drugs. They are the youthful rebels of the angelic realm, and don't mind staying up very late at night.

Cherubs: Angels in diapers.

ANGER

Anger is the most important human emotion. The purpose of all **therapy** is to get in touch with your anger. People who have no anger to get in touch with cannot be helped even by the most profound and expensive therapy.

By far the most daring work that has been carried out in the field of anger must be the ground-breakingly innovative 'Getting-in-Touch-with-Your-Anger Workshops' led by Thwaite and Brittle in the early 1960s. Two hundred eager participants would pay the somewhat steep fee in advance, and then turn up for the weekend at the appointed venue. After an hour or two they would begin to wonder why no organisers or workshop leaders had turned up. No one *was* going to turn up, in fact — all weekend. By about lunch time on the first day the workshop would already be starting to work extremely well.

AQUAHOLICS

Addicts of **mineral water**. Aquaholics Anonymous is now the largest (and also most secretive) addiction organisation in the western world.

AQUAPHOBIA

Fear of mineral water (well-justified, it appears, judging from the size of Aquaholics Anonymous).

AQUAPUNCTURE

Underwater Chinese healing art.

ARCHETYPE

Nobody actually knows what this word means, but it is now so widely used that no one can afford to admit that. Other similar terms: paradigm, process and gestalt.

ASSERTIVENESS

Being rude.

ASTRAL TRAVEL

Journeying of the spirit without taking the body along (see **Out of body experience**).

It is now fashionable to use the word astral in almost any context, as in Astral Projection, Astral Plane and Astral Sex. Astral Projection is a kind of cosmic slide show. Astral Sex means doing it during an **out-of-body** experience. The prime 'user's manual' on Astral Sex is R. Bach's *The Bridge Across Forever*. A particularly exciting place to have Astral Sex is on an Astral Plane. Especially with an Astral Air Hostess (or Host). Some people say that Astral Orgasm is 'a bit of a non-event'.

Another popular activity these days is Astral Study,

where the student's spirit leaves the body during sleep and journeys to etheric workshops, where they can study esoteric teachings with such great teachers and leading authorities as Jesus Christ, Shakyamuni Buddha or Mohammed.

Course content tends to range over such enduring material as moving of mountains, saving the world in five easy lessons and advanced transubstantiation. The only problem is that the students aren't allowed to remember what they have learned when they return to their normal state. The information stays in the unconscious and remains the property of the course organisers.

Other popular astral pursuits include Astral Stamp Collecting, Astral Trainspotting, Astral Gardening and Astral Washing Up.

ASTROLOGY

Astrology is the study of how human beings are affected by the influences of complex cosmic phenomena such as the movement of planets, especially around the time of birth. The analysis of these influences enables prediction of what people will be like and how their future will unfold.

Astrology is an extremely variegated science, as old as time itself. There are a great number of different forms of astrology, and each one will render different and usually conflicting prognostications for any one individual. For instance, there is Western Zodiac Astrology, Egyptian Astrology, Sumerian Astrology, Inca and Aztec Astrology, Cabbalist Astrology, Intuitive Astrology and Tabloid Newspaper Astrology (which is not really a form of astrology at all, but a primitive way of flattering readers).

There are also different qualities of astrology: Mundane

BUS STOP ASTROLOGY

Yep! we jump in where other fools fear to tread...

ARIES

Astrology, Quite Interesting Astrology and Absolutely Fascinating Astrology. And astrology can be applied to all kinds of specialist subjects — as, for instance, in Houseplant Astrology, Traffic-on-Roads Astrology or Jam-Making Astrology. There is even a whole range of forms which specialise in predictions specifically for animals,

most notably the Classical Chinese form, but also the Tibetan variety (for llamas) and Mesozoic Astrology, which was designed for dinosaurs; unfortunately the latter never really took off.

In Western Zodiac Astrology, the following descriptions apply to the twelve 'signs', or types of people, according to date of birth. These influences are absolutely fixed and exactly the same for everyone of that sign, and there is no getting away from what they say.

ARIES (21 March - 20 April)

People born under this sign are extraordinarily dynamic, fearless, confident and action-oriented. With their incredible drive, overriding ambition and unstoppable, bursting energy, they make terribly good human cannon-balls for old-fashioned circuses.

TAURUS (21 April - 21 May)

Taureans are only interested in food, sex, beauty, wealth, and generally getting their own way. But they are also fond of making sweeping statements that seem to be very profound and meaningful, which upon closer examination prove not to say anything at all; this is why they belong under the sign of the Bull.

Taureans tend to be extremely stubborn, and they often experience negativity and anger, especially later on in life when they discover that they will not be able to take their prized possessions with them into their next *incarnation*.

GEMINI (22 May - 21 June)

Gemini people are those for whom things can always go either way, especially when any choice of options is involved. This particularly applies to making decisions for themselves, when they frequently become paralysed by inner conflict.

However, Geminis are also intelligent, quick-thinking and good at communication. This means that they are able to get excellent jobs that involve giving instructions to others, while they can still keep changing their minds about what they want those people to do. When you see someone directing a group of people at a large hole in the road, for example, and they constantly come back to dig it up again for another purpose, then it's probably a Gemini in charge.

CANCER (22 June - 23 July)

Cancerians are very vulnerable beings who are — quite rightly — cautious about how they live their lives. Cancerians should be careful not to travel long distances, move about too quickly, or go too far in a straight line. They must follow all advice that they are given. They should be particularly vigilant around sophisticated or complex technical apparatus such as high-powered computers, nuclear particle accelerators and ball-point pens. Even when the Cancerian does exercise extreme caution, things can still go terribly wrong. The most important thing of all for them is not to panic.

People born under this sign are very good hermit material.

CANCER

LEO (24 July - 23 August)

Leos have very large egos; they are ostentatious, arrogant, land pushy; they are highly successful denizens of the urban jungle. Leos make excellent cheats and liars.

Many of them are easy to spot, because of having their shirt open to the waist, showing lots of chest hair and wearing a big gold medallion. The men tend to show themselves off a bit, too.

LEO

Worrying comes very naturally to Virgos; even Freud considered them to be particularly anally retentive. If you invite them into your home, they will pick up tiny bits of fluff from your carpet, or untangle your twisted telephone cord. Virgos are especially fond of medicines: when they go on holiday, they will take an extra suitcase just for remedies. Doctors, chemists and pharmacists are known to keep the phone numbers of nearby Virgo customers for emergency use, in case they suddenly run out of something that a customer might need late at night.

Although blind to their own faults and fierce in their resistance to criticism, Virgos are intensely demanding and hypercritical of others. No partner of a Virgo has ever developed dandruff and stayed in the relationship. In romance they are extremely exacting — especially in bed. This is why so many Virgos are single; and anyway they do make very good spinsters and bachelors.

LIBRA (24 September - 23 October)
Most people like Librans; they are kind, fair-minded and full of consideration for others. They are blessed with a strong sense of harmony and equilibrium, which is a joy for others around them to experience.

However, in their eagerness to preserve equanimity, maintain balance and avoid conflict, Librans often seem loath to adhere to any fixed position or express any strongly-held point of view. Yet if someone else hazards an opinion or makes a generalisation, they will immediately

VIRGO (24 August - 23 September)
Virgo people are scrupulous and meticulous perfectionists. They are not a good choice if you want to take someone out for the evening because they take so long to get ready, and they will also look at themselves in every shop window along the way to check that they still look okay. They always know what time it is, and carry a Thesaurus around with them at all times. Virgos take more showers and baths than all the other signs put together.

LIBRA

argue against it, on principle. Trying to get them to decide where to go for a picnic, and what to bring along, is worse still. Come to think of it, most people dislike Librans intensely.

SCORPIO (24 October - 22 November)

Nobody likes Scorpios, who really aren't interested in very much besides pain and sex. They usually become **Rolfers** or **Primal Integration** therapists.

SAGITTARIUS (23 November - 22 December)

Sagittarians have that combination of far-reaching vision and ceaseless activity which means that they cannot look at a horizon without wanting to head straight for it, especially at sunset. What with their natural generosity, this means that they make the very best Lone Rangers. At the same time, Sagittarians should *not* join the police, for their itinerant nature means that they have far too much natural sympathy for **Travellers**.

(If a Tonto is sought for a Sagittarian Lone Ranger, a Navajo **Aquarian** would be an ideal choice.)

SAGITTARIUS

> you always seem slightly detached dear..

> CLANK,

> CLANK!

AQUARIUS

CAPRICORN (22 December - 20 January)

Capricorns excel at anything to do with imposing structure, maintaining control and stressing the importance of the 'usefulness' of everything. Thus they make excellent men. Jesus Christ, for instance, was a man.

AQUARIUS (21 January - 19 February)

As all Aquarians are aware, they are truly wonderful human beings, full of deservingness for the benefits that are bounteously showered upon them by the universe. They are magnets forever drawing to themselves abundance, well-being, love and happiness. They know that the Divine Essence flows through them constantly.

They are always aware which crystal to wear, what *ley line* to follow, and which is their lucky kitchen utensil. Aquarians live on an altogether different plane from regular mortals, from whom they seem somewhat detached and to whom they often seem a bit of a pain. If Aquarians ever grow up, they become professional health-food faddists, *UFO spotters* or psychic brain surgeons with no clients.

PISCES (20 February - 20 March)

Pisceans are very good at 'going with the flow'. They also possess two somewhat embarrassing traits — they are full of gushing emotion and they are fond of martyring themselves. But the possession of these three qualities does make them extremely popular as partners or spouses; for if you share your life with a Piscean, they will: a) always go along with what you want; b) make you feel loved; and c) if they do martyr themselves, you can always cash in the life insurance. *And* they like suffering! So Scorpio/Pisces is the perfect romantic match.

Pisceans often think that they are very mysterious, but actually they're just rather uninteresting. They would all sign up for Assertiveness Training, only they don't want to cause anyone any trouble.

ASTROLOGICAL FOOTNOTE

The above accounts, of course, only refer to Sun Signs. In order to complete a person's full 'Natal Chart', many other criteria must also be taken into account, including Moon Signs, Mutable Signs, Immutable Signs, Plus Signs, Minus Signs, Traffic Signs and Signs of the Times.

AURA

The pioneering *Concise Dictionary of New Age Blather* (Dublin University Press, 1899) defines the aura as 'a wishy-washy, etheric kind of an energy-field type of a thing, which sort of surrounds the body, as you might say'. Use of the term has since been extended to refer to anything that has this vague quality, or that no one is sure about, or that might not exist or might not happen, or indeed may only be a substitute for something else. Hence, an aural phone message is one which the recipient says he will pass on to the right person, but will instead immediately forget because he hasn't written it down. Aural contraception is what which, as often as not, one forgets to take; and so on. Likewise aural tradition, aural sex etc etc.

AVATAR

A kind of Eastern celestial deity that has taken an imperfect human incarnate form on earth — lit. 'aviator who has lost an eye'.

BACH FLOWER REMEDIES

Essences of flowers and other plants that miraculously make all kinds of unpleasant emotional states disappear immediately, without you doing anything else about it.

BACH FLOWER MUSIC

Music to listen to while taking Bach Flower Remedies.

BIODYNAMIC GROWING

Cultivation method that concentrates the earth's vital energies into plants, making organic growing, by comparison, pale into pathetic insignificance. Biodynamic vegetables have so much energy that they are very restless and never stay for long where they were planted; they move around a great deal, especially during the night. Fierce disputes between growers, and even fatalities, have arisen when vegetables have leapt into neighbouring farmers' fields.

BIRTHING

Pompous term for 'giving birth'.

BREATHE

Slang for a *rebirthing* session, as in "I'm just off for a breathe now."

Bach Flower Remedy LIQUEUR CHOCS

ROCK ROSE - PANIC!
STAR OF BETHLEHEM - FRIGHT
WILD OAT - PATH IN LIFE
SWEET CHESTNUT - DEJECTION
WALNUT - ADJUSTMENT
GORSE - PESSIMISM
HONEYSUCKLE - HOMESICKNESS
CRAB APPLE - SELF DISGUST
AGRIMONY - ADDICTION: CHOCOLATE

CHAKRAS

The body's internal centres or vortices of dynamic energy and excitement, cultivated since time immemorial by Indian yogis. The English name actually arrived as an ethnic mispronunciation of the word 'chocolate' which, when it was introduced to the Indian sub-continent last century, was found to produce almost identical sensations of energy, dynamism and excitement, only about sixty years more quickly.

Each chakra governs a different area of our lives, and has its own colour, frequency of energy vibration, corresponding flower, favourite TV station — and even its own affirmation, e.g. base chakra: "My anus is my friend."

CHANGE

See *Growth*

CHANNELLING

An esoteric method whereby a disembodied voice is brought through from the realm of spirit, usually via a person whose consciousness has vacated his or her own body. The term is derived from that used to describe the habit of switching a television set rapidly between stations, performed by the same kind of vacant individuals in a similar trance-like state.

Channelling ancient warrior spirits has become very popular among housewives and young children since they showed how to do it on the popular children's TV programme 'Blue Peter'.

CHANTING

See *Nam-myo-ho-renge-kyo*

CHIROPRACTIC

An incredibly clever, inventive and lucrative form of physical *therapy*, which came up with a brilliant ploy to ensure continuing demand. A bill would be supplied at the end of a successful course of treatment, which would be of such an astronomical nature that the client would experience spontaneous whiplash and thus be obliged to sign up for several additional sessions.

COLONIC IRRIGATION

A sophisticated form of internal bodily agriculture whose main aim, apparently, is to provide a constant supply of fluids to meet the needs of intestinal flora. Recent obsession with the activity has been so extreme, however, that the lives of some enthusiasts have been threatened by distended bowels. Rapid over-evolution of species in the internal environment, too, can be an even more serious problem; these may include not only flora but fauna too,

with first herbivorous animals and then carnivores. Presence of this latter tends to cause extremely severe abdominal pains and constipation. Don't try this at home.

COMMUNICATION

Communication is a vital New Age concept, recently re-invented to suit the spirit of this age; New-Agers believe that no one really communicated before them. Here are one or two particularly useful types of communication, with helpful examples.

General purpose New Age communications (and what they really mean):

"I really like where you're coming from." (Maybe we can get together some time.)

"I have this really strong feeling that we met in a past lifetime." (I'd like to have sex with you.)

"My soul-mate really doesn't understand me." (I'd *very much* like to have sex with you.)

"I'd very much like to have sex with you." (I'm incredibly liberated, evolved and terribly up-front.)

"My life is really working now." (I'm still in a mess.)

"Tarquin and I are really working out our problems now." (We're both in a mess.)

"Kevin has got really weird energy." (He smells.)

"I really hear what you're saying." (I can't get a word in edgeways.)

Things to say to people when they're feeling bad and you want them to feel even worse.

Some traditional communications for this situation:

"I understand how you must feel."

"Sometimes things have to get worse before they get better."

"Every cloud has a silver lining."

"Look at all the things you have to be grateful for!"

Some New Age versions that work even better:

"I had a feeling something like this was going to happen."

"How did you manage to manifest that in your life?"

"You'll really grow from this experience."

"From our darkest moments come our brightest treasures."

"It's probably just your karma."

COMMUNITY

Any group of people whose *karma* is to live together because they don't get on very well with each other. See also *Findhorn*.

COMPLEMENTARY MEDICINE

1. Holistic health practices which consciously seek to work *with*, rather than in opposition *to*, modern western scientific allopathic medicine, eg non-toxic dental fillings, chiropractic or Hopi Ear-Nose-and-Throat Candles.

2. Holistic health practices where the practitioner says really nice things to you, such as "That's a nice tie you're wearing today, Mr Smith", "I must say, that jacket really suits you, Mr Brown", or "Well, Mrs Jones, there doesn't seem to be a thing wrong with you; that'll be £55 please."

CONSCIOUSNESS

Consciousness is another term which no one knows the meaning of, but it's still a good word to use a lot; no one will ever dream of asking you what it means.

COUNSELLING

Form of *therapy* where someone with a lot of problems goes to someone who has so many more problems that they will put up with the job of listening to the first person talk about their problems. There are many different forms, such as Client-Centred Counselling, Counsellor-Centred Counselling and Confectionery-Centred Counselling. But perhaps the most bizarre is Relationship Counselling.

Relationship counselling is very helpful to couples who are experiencing difficulty in their relationship, through providing resources that cannot be obtained within the relationship itself. For instance, each person in the relationship can come in separately to see a counsellor, and spend a whole hour complaining about the other person, and know that they will be listened to with total attention and without the slightest objection or interruption.

Some counsellors even let both partners come in at the same time and yell at each other. This is done without embarrassment, disapproval or telling either of them how ridiculous they are being.

CROP (or CORN) CIRCLES

Corn circles first began to appear spontaneously in south-west England during the early 1990s, and have since 'cropped up' increasingly throughout the British Isles, Europe, the USA and indeed around the rest of the world. They usually appear in cereal crop fields, with the corn flattened in a characteristic spiral pattern. The circles are always found in the vicinity of important earth **power points**, especially at the intersection of major **ley lines**.

With the passing of each year, however, the patterns created by this mysterious phenomenon have progressed, becoming more and more elaborate and esoteric, with

increasingly complex geometrical content that seems to draw upon ancient sacred graphics. The most talked-about recent examples have been the elaborate Egyptian fertility mandala which appeared near Silbury Hill in 1992, the enormous and complex 1993 Aztec Calendar at Avebury, the extensive Sperm Cluster motif of the same year that surrounded Stonehenge, and the Small Swirly Thing on Mr Bickering's front lawn at 27 Myrtle Avenue, Totnes. They always appear during the night.

Various explanations for the creation of these enigmatic phenomena have been put forward, but most sensible people agree that they are the landing or take-off sites for alien spacecraft or **UFOs**; for they are invariably accompanied by sightings of Flying Saucers and other luminosities, and are usually followed next morning by the discovery of leftovers from extra-terrestrial picnics. Few observers doubt that NASA is involved, and there is clearly a huge cover-up conspiracy by the CIA, MI6, the Kremlin and

the entire global military-industrial complex. It is also generally accepted that some benign but determined force is at work, as evidenced by the numerous alien abductions of individuals who have been caught trying to create hoax circles.

Other explanations that have been put forward for the creation of these compositions include unusual wind

patterns, low-temperature ball lightning, or animals (giant hedgehogs, badgers or rutting pheasants). In the vicinity of Dartmoor in the west of England, the creator is widely held to be an escaped puma that walks round in circles before lying down to rest for the night.

But whatever the method of creation, there must be some ultimate, higher purpose behind their appearance. It may indeed be that we are now on the verge of cracking the comprehensive code that will explain the precise meaning of all of these diverse compositions; and when we do, Mr Bickering believes, we will be able to tap into a vast, cosmic pool of long-lost knowledge on gardening.

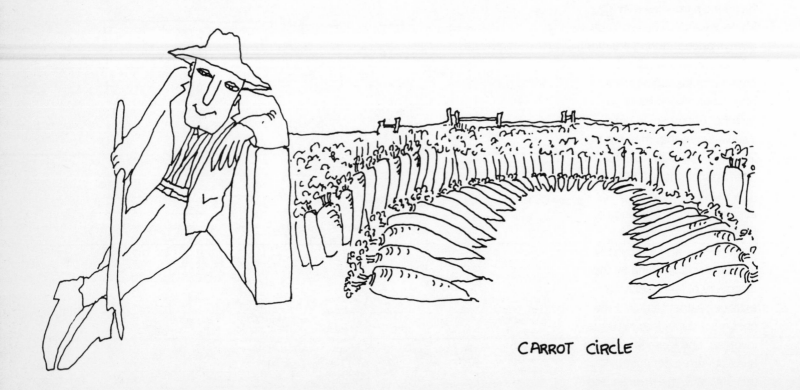

CARROT CIRCLE

CRYSTAL HEALING

The systematic destruction of the earth's subterranean store of minerals, as well as the overlying fields, hills and mountains in the process, through ever-increasing mining operations in developing countries, so that a few practitioners in 'developed' countries can use the energies of these crystals to 'heal the planet'.

CRUSTIE

See **Traveller**.

EVAS

See *Fairies*.

DOLPHINS

Dolphins have been very unfashionable until recently; people used to think of them as big fish that can't even breathe underwater. But we are at last beginning to realise that they are something very much more special than that. Dolphins are, in fact, aliens that came to our planet millions of years ago from another galaxy. They did this in order to be ready to help us here on earth much later, with a major disaster that they foresaw humankind bringing upon itself and the planet around the late twentieth century AD. These aliens realised, all those millions of years ago, that we would run out of ideas for things to make into china mantelpiece ornaments. And sure enough, when the late twentieth century came, we really went for the idea of dolphins.

Dolphins are extremely intelligent, with very highly developed sensory perception and insight, and this is undoubtedly why they did not choose to manifest on the earth as human-type beings.

DOWSING

A traditional method of divination, originally used exclusively for finding underground water, but now widely fashionable as an aid to locating ley lines, bad energy or a long-lost soul-mate — or indeed to assist in any kind of decision-making. Rather than the old-fashioned forked hazel stick, current popular tools include anything that moves, bends or swings like a pendulum; most-used items today are the ubiquitous pair of coat-hangers, or a herb teabag on a string, if one is in a cafe at the time. True to its roots, however, the people most attracted to this oracular method still seem to be the watery types who are inherently unable to make up their minds for themselves, and indeed the term 'dowsing' is thought to refer to the habitual state of sleepy stupor which seems to call for constant divination in the first place.

E_{CK}

Archetypal cry of existential despair or disgust.

ECOLOGICAL AWARENESS

See **Green**

EDUCATION

An archaic, patriarchal, authoritarian system designed to reduce the capabilities of children so that they will be able to cope with living in society as adults.

EINSTEIN

See **Physics**.

ELEMENTS

An analytical cosmological tool used to divide the entirety of phenomenological reality into four or five simple categories, for reasons as yet unknown. There are an enormous number of systems which have evolved for this purpose, varying greatly from culture to culture and from age to age; however, they all have one feature in common, viz. each system believes that it is the only correct one. Here are a few of the most significant:

Western Zodiac 4 Elements System: Fire, Air, Earth and Water
Classical Chinese 5 Elements System: Fire, Earth, Water, Wood and Metal
Ancient Irish 7 Elements System: Stick, Stone, Bog, Bone, Drink, Talk and String.

This little-known latter system was passed down orally from ancient times and first set down in writing by St Patrick, but was successfully suppressed by the Vatican who took the early Irish Christian cosmologists by surprise by inventing the Spanish Inquisition and sending it to Ireland to quell this very heresy.

ENERGY

The perfect item of jargon, and the most used word in the New Age. Pioneered by Einstein, energy simply means 'anything that exists'.

ENLIGHTENMENT

Realisation, development of the qualities of the Buddha, or achievement of the Nirvana state; not as big a deal these days as it once was.

ENLIGHTENED MASTERS

Masters who have achieved a state of *enlightenment*. Enlightened masters were very special beings who have been traditionally revered among lesser mortals, and given very special names that indicate their high status and the long time spent on their path to enlightenment. The names also convey something of the individuality of each one's particular mode of achieving their advanced state. These names are recognisable because they always end the same way. Thus 'Yogananda' means 'He who becomes enlightened through the pursuit of complicated postures'. Likewise 'Lotusananda' is 'One who achieves self-realisation through sitting for countless aeons by an ornamental pond'.

Nowadays, however, due to wider Western interest in the East and in spiritual matters in general, there is a very great and ever-increasing number of Enlightened Masters.

Furthermore, it is becoming more and more difficult to find a new and individual spiritual name for each one. Consequently, as the path to enlightenment seems to get shorter and shorter, these names tend to get longer and longer — rather like motor vehicle registrations or telephone numbers — though this does often add a certain charm. Hence titles such as 'Tantramananda' — 'Young acolyte who travels the path of Righteous Anger', or 'Hamaneggananda' — 'Bodhisattva of Very Great Appetite'. Likewise also Rescuremananda, Handymanananda and even Bananaramananda.

ESSENTIAL OILS

Those oils used in aromatherapy which represent the bare minimum a therapist can get away with using because, since this therapy has become incredibly marketable, the oils have also become incredibly expensive.

Family

A group of people who have even more intense *karma*
around each other than a *community*.

FEELINGS

Another word for emotions. Women have always had feelings, but men did not start having them until the 1970s (see **Men's work**).

FENG SHUI (pron. 'fung shway')

A type of Chinese mushroom used in soups and herbal remedies.

FILOFAX

Popular cultural icon of the 1980s. Anthropologists of the future will probably provide a definition such as this:

The distinguishing tool, developed in the late twentieth century AD, of Homo Filofaxus. It was, for a short time, the status symbol *par excellence* of this fanatically organisation-conscious culture, and featured prominently in rituals and mating displays; a big fat one was especially prized by the male of the species. The true strain H. Filofaxus rapidly degenerated into many different hybridised sub-species such as H. Lefaxus, H. Ryman Filofaxus, H. WHSmithsus, and H. Cheapus Plasticus. The whole race eventually died out as a result of bitter internecine warfare on a global scale between the diametrically opposed factions H. Filofaxophilus and H. Filofaxophobus.

FINDHORN

Perhaps the best-known of the New Age communities, which grew up at a remote and unlikely location of this name, in the far north of Scotland.

It all started back in 1962. A couple of very ordinary people, who have gone down in history only as Uncle Peter and Auntie Eileen, are said to have visited the area on a golfing holiday, staying in a small caravan at the local campsite, together with a mysterious third person. At the end of their holiday the three people, who all very much enjoyed difficulties and suffering, decided on a sudden mad impulse that they would like to stay on in this desolate spot, make it their home, and start having children so as to make the tiny caravan even more crowded than it was already. As soon as this deeply instinctive decision was taken, all three unexpectedly discovered that they were each able to obtain inner guidance from supernatural sources, which enabled them to tell each of the two *other* members of the party what they were 'supposed' to be doing in this strange place. It was this pattern of vicarious direction-finding, in fact, that has characterised almost the whole development of the project ever since.

Uncle Peter would get his guidance for the others while out walking by himself in the far-off snowy mountains, and Aunt Eileen, for reasons still unknown, got her messages at night, while sitting on the toilet. But the mysterious other person had a more radical source — the entire body of spirits that locally inhabited the realm of plants. All three of them had their own respective areas of expertise and practical responsibility: Uncle Peter enjoyed gardening and getting married to people; Aunt Eileen was very good at channelling, and was in fact the first person to do it in horn-rimmed spectacles; and the mysterious other person (nicknamed Mop) was excellent at being mysterious. Indeed it was her mysterious communications with the entities of the plant realm that were to have the most important bearing on the Findhorn Community's immediate development. As a result of the messages she received, she was able to give Uncle Peter uncannily helpful instructions on gardening, and Aunt Eileen penetrating insights into flower arranging.

In fact, it was Mop's plant-spirit contacts that directly led to the unlikely success and unexpected fame of the Findhorn phenomenon. Every day she would commune outdoors with these normally unseen 'wee folk' that govern how things grow — elves, pixies, devas and many other kinds of fairies. Then she would go straight to Uncle Peter and set him to work putting into practice the subtle wisdom which she had gleaned. The results were extraordinary. Even though the site was bleak and barren, with practically no soil and with bitter winds that blew in from the North Pole even in summer, vegetables in the garden grew abundantly — and to immense proportions. Soon there were cabbages that were ten feet across, pumpkins that you could practically live in, and enchanted forests of broccoli.

Naturally word soon spread, and people of spiritual bent flocked in to see these wonders for themselves. Many visitors, accepting Aunt Eileen's still-flowing guidance, rented adjacent caravans and settled down to help consume and tend the ever-swelling fruits of the earth. These people formed the fledgling community, which proceeded to expand by leaps and bounds. Even horticultural deities and other related entities would come to visit — Pan dropped in from time to time, giving valuable hints on developing a 'wild garden', and Bacchus tried to tempt Uncle Peter into viniculture and barley cultivation for the production of malt whisky. It is probably just as well that the whole community was vegetarian, with no need for animal husbandry, or goodness knows what monstrous creations might have evolved.

Throughout the 1960s the community's reputation grew, and its founding-figures became recognised world leaders in the triple fields of innovation that they had pioneered — producing horticultural wonders, attracting people to live in a technically uninhabitable environment (with the nearest cinema over 200 miles away) and getting divine indications as to how other people than oneself should behave. Everyone in the world who remotely needed to make progress on any of these issues came and settled down here, for a short while at least. The Findhorn Community had become a sort of continentally-displaced giant ashram.

At this point, however, an unexpected change in direction was forced upon the community, brought about by a sudden outbreak of pests at the end of the 60s, which soon got a hold on all the main crops. Nor were these any ordinary pests — there were pumpkin weevils the size of tortoises, earwigs that could easily nip your hand off at the wrist, and a horrific plague of killer cabbage-white butterflies. The Garden Pest Devas were duly consulted by Mop, and the infallible word was passed on to Uncle Peter that it was time for the community to 'start cultivating people rather than vegetables'. It was at this point that Uncle Peter realised that his work at Findhorn was complete, and he went off to seek his fortune in America. Soon after this, too, Mop left to live on some far-flung urban allotment, without even leaving a forwarding address. Now there was only Aunt Eileen to tell everyone what they should be doing.

But cultivation of people certainly took place. So many joined the community in the 70s that physical expansion was necessary too. After acquiring the caravan park itself, the Findhorn Foundation began to absorb adjacent local houses, farms and then hotels. Yet more people came, and nearby villages began to be swallowed up, then towns and one or two whole counties. Alongside this rampant physical expansion, the Findhorn Community began to spawn other communities that imitated it, all over the world. The guidance, in fact, said that the Findhorn Community was to expand into no less than a 'Planetary Village', and so that was what everyone was going for; the community was clearly meant to grow to cover the whole planet. Aunt Eileen was so busy giving guidance to everyone that she hardly ever left the toilet.

Further afield still, the tiny island of Erraid was purchased, followed by a plethora of other insular acquisitions, starting with nearby Iona and then Mull. Negotiations then began for the accession of the Inner and Outer Hebrides and the Orkneys as a comprehensive package. At the same time, and even more ambitiously, plans were being put in hand for taking over the whole of Ireland, but the Ulster Unionists put a spanner in the works — they wouldn't recognise anyone's guidance but their own. The Findhorn Community authorities were completely inexperienced in dealing such an approach.

The departure of the authoritative founding-father, Uncle Peter, had shaken the community more than was probably realised at the time. Furthermore, as soon as he left, an alien virus of democratic decision-making insidiously began to infect this tight-knit society. By the early 80s this had reached epidemic proportions, and soon almost everyone was doing what they themselves wanted to do, rather than what someone else's guidance dictated. So when westward expansion came up against the Loyalist Ulster obstacle, latent doubts about community policy started coming to the surface, and everything began to be questioned — even the fundamental concept of spiritual expansion and world domination. Aunt Eileen even stopped giving guidance, and came out of the toilet.

People began to say that the true essence of the native form of Christianity had been forgotten in all this. Puritanical ethicism, the fundamental concept of the difficulty of life, and guilt about success needed to be established as the core of policy-making. Life was too easy. The institution of interminable democratic meetings was brought in around this time, and this, together with the questioning of success and enjoyment, proved extremely successful in producing a turnaround in the community's affairs; no decision on any matter of business or action was taken for the best part of ten years. It was in this period, and especially the late 80s, that the community also began to create forms of communication that would further hinder progress and the imparting of meaning. This linguistic development has been a vital part of the Findhorn Community's legacy to New Age and spiritual groups the world over. Classic terms such as 'process', 'manifestation' and 'focaliser' can still be heard in some third-world countries today. Another device was to totally ban the use of excessively straightforward words that might aid decision-making or progress, such as 'can/can't', 'either/or' and 'mistake'.

At the Findhorn Community in the 90s, however, the pendulum has swung the other way again. After focusing on first vegetable, then spiritual and physical growth, the emphasis has now officially transferred to financial growth. Nevertheless, even in putting this new policy into action, certain distinctive Findhorn traditions remain essentially unchanged — the customs of looking to discredited ways from the past for inspiration, of rejecting conventional wisdom and of obtaining guidance from unlikely entities that live on another plane. Hence the entry of the community into its Thatcherite phase. The Findhorn Community began to privatise itself like mad and hive off a plethora of lean, thrusting young market-oriented capitalist ventures. These include cult books and magazines, addictive board games, esoteric videos, cutting-edge computer software and fashion-conscious building design ventures — all ready and willing to compete in the ruthless cut-throat world of healing and enlightenment as it exists today.

But some things never change. Aunt Eileen still has her horn-rimmed glasses.

FLOAT

A pretentious term for a session spent at the flotarium, as in "I had a great float today!" This term is used by people who also use expressions like "having a breathe" or "I'm in a really good space right now", esp. *rebirthers*.

FREUD

Sigmund Freud (b.1856) became famous for his personal work in obsessional neurosis. Widely regarded as the Father of Modern Psychoanalysis, for instance, Freud became convinced that the Son of Mod. Psych. wanted to kill him, due to infatuation with the Mother of Mod. Psych.

Freud lived in Vienna, where he attracted many famous clients to his practice. One of these was the author James Joyce, who had left Dublin upon being told that he ought 'to get his head examined'. But after seven years Freud upset Joyce by opining that his writing was merely a disguised manifestation of repressed sexual desire. Joyce responded by switching to Freud's most famous student psychoanalyst. Freud was never to forgive Joyce, especially when he later published the book that immortalised this transfer of psychiatric allegiance, *Portrait of the Artist as a Jung Man*.

GAIA

Very trendy name for girls born after c. 1987.

GOALS

Things that footballers score, as in "Western society is becoming more and more materialistic and goal-orientated."

GREEN

A colour got by mixing yellow and blue.

GROUNDED

A highly complementary adjective, as in "So-and-so is very grounded." This, for reasons unknown, is a seemingly desirable way for people to be, implying perhaps connectedness with the earth rather than the sky. In practice, due to gravity, just about everyone is grounded.

GROWTH

As in "I feel I'm really growing from this experience." Personal Growth was a middle-class social phenomenon which gained much credence in the 1970s and 80s. It was the spiritual component of what was then known as the Yuppie movement, and was the preferred spiritual path of the same people, who had grown accustomed to expecting the value of their homes, property and stock market shares to keep going up and up for ever. As the crash came, and advertisers of investment plans were obliged to point out to potential customers that 'values can go down as well as up', the same was realised about the form of 'spiritual materialism' known as Personal Growth. Unfortunately, as a direct consequence of this, there is now a whole class of individuals who are probably permanently trapped in Personal Negative Equity (or 'Personal Shrinkage').

References:
R. Wiseman, Dynamo Press, 1984: *How to Change Your Life*.
R. Wiseman, Dynamo Press, 1985: *How to Change Your Life Even More*.
R. Wiseman, Dynamo Press, 1986: *How to Change Your Life Back to How it Was Before, Because Actually Maybe it Wasn't So Bad After All*.

ARA

(See also **Chakra**) The major body energy centre, acupressure point and meditation focal area, found near the navel. It is named after its discoverer, Matt O'Hara, a celebrated World War 1 spy, whose colourful career ended abruptly when he was captured and shot in this very spot by a firing squad personally supervised by Adolf Hitler. O'Hara himself was an extremely interesting and charismatic figure, a shameless and irresistible womaniser whose code-name was 'Scarlet'. It was he, in fact, who semi-posthumously coined the term 'homme fatale', referring to the mantra 'OM' which he was uttering at the moment of his unfortunate demise by shooting.

HAY DIET

A currently faddish way of eating, also known as food combining, that says you musn't eat anything like fish and chips, meat and potatoes, or beef and stroganoff together in the same meal, and that the ideal diet for human beings is dried grass on its own.

HAY FEVER

An endemic urge to follow the teachings of one Louise Hay, pioneer of studies into the mental, emotional and metaphysical causes of disease. Hay is author of a string of best-selling titles, starting with the now out-of-print *You Can Heal Your Finger* and followed by *You Can Heal Your Body*, *You Can Heal Your Car*, . . . *Your Life* . . . *Your Bank Balance* . . . *The World*, and numerous other classics.

HEALING

Making people better.

ABSENT HEALING: Healing which hasn't worked.

HEALING CRISIS: Healing which has made someone worse rather than better.

HERB TEAS

At one time, herb teas actually meant 'teas made from herbs'. Even after the advent of the tea bag, you could still find such honest, down-to-earth, homely favourites as Camomile Tea, Mixed Fruit Tea or the slightly more adventurous Rosehip and Hibiscus. You knew, more or less, what you were getting.

Sometime in the 80s, however, herb teas began to be discovered by ordinary people and not just hippies and oddball health freaks. It was suddenly okay to ask for something other than interminable cups of regular tea, even when visiting the homes of relative strangers. What was actually happening was that business moguls in remote executive suites had suddenly begun to take notice and recognise a whole new, highly lucrative potential market. Almost overnight the old-fashioned and modestly successful little wholefood herb-tea companies were swallowed whole by the giant food conglomerates. And just as suddenly the old products weren't considered exciting or exotic enough, and a whole new generation of bizarrely-named items hit the shelves of every supermarket in the land. By now, of course, some of the hippies and oddballs had become marketing directors, and this psychedelic influence was clearly reflected in the names of the plethora of new teas: Purple Zinger, Tangerine Trip, Rhubarb Rendezvous, Celestial Stardust — that sort of thing. It just went on and on, and there was very little way of knowing what you were getting. What was being sold, in fact, was not so much a beverage as a desirable image, a kind of vaguely-defined mood. And an expensive mood at that.

But the most recent research conducted by the advertising agencies representing the food giants has shown something which took all of them completely by surprise. They discovered that, despite the incredible demand and the huge amounts of revenue generated, people don't actually *like* herb tea. Herb teas are *still* universally perceived as 'uninteresting', 'insipid', 'unstimulating' and 'dead boring'. The crux of the problem, they realised, is that drinks which don't have powerful, unnatural, harmful or dangerous ingredients just don't have any appeal. They don't 'do' anything for you. So the sales

people reckoned that if they could do as well as they had been doing with products that people don't even like, just think how much more they could sell of beverages which actually delivered some goods.

And now a new generation of teas is in the production line; they are not the likes of their lovey-dovey, namby-pamby, wimpy predecessors — they are a leaner, meaner bunch altogether. They are definitely more earthed, focusing on the genuine creation of particular states of mind or body, using whatever type of synthetic or chemical additives are necessary. For the research also showed that people 'trust' anything that can be called herb tea, and don't bother to read the list of ingredients. These teas are more effective, or at least more dangerous-sounding. And the names will make this point very clearly: Kaffeine Kickstart; Orange Aggressor; Fungal Faze-out. And perhaps the gentlest one of the bunch is Prune Persuader.

HERBACEOUS BORDER
Vegetarian lodger who enjoys gardening.

HOLISTIC
An adjective meaning flaky, off-the-wall or ill-thought-out; literally 'full of holes'. As in 'holistic healing', 'holistic approach', 'very holistic', 'totally holistic', 'incredibly holistic' etc.

HUGGING

A highly contagious disease which has now reached epidemic proportions. It is thought to have begun in the late 70s, when people went in for a lot of promiscuous, unprotected *chakra*-connecting with complete strangers. People who are HUG-positive usually develop full-blown sentimentality within a matter of months.

HUNDREDTH MONKEY

This is an attractively esoteric New Age expression, which cannot fail to impress your friends if you casually let it drop from time to time. Hardly anyone can hear it mentioned without asking what it means. If they do, however, it is important not to tell them, so that it remains elitist and mysterious.

The term refers to a particular anthropological phenomenon that has enormous significance for the evolution of human consciousness, and our ability to find better ways of living on the planet. It was discovered quite accidentally on a Pacific archipelago, which had relatively recently been colonised by a particular species of monkey. Scientists saw this as a unique opportunity to discover how a species would adapt to an unfamiliar environment.

The monkeys focused on coconuts as the most available food source, and found a reasonable supply that had broken open by falling from the trees. But when this supply was limited, some monkeys began to experiment with ways of dealing with those that were still intact. After some months, an enterprising individual on one of the islands was observed to discover that a particular type of sharp stone would do the trick. In the coming weeks, other monkeys on that island began to imitate the pioneer.

Now, at the moment when around one hundred monkeys were using the technique, the rest of the monkeys on that island began to use it — all at once. But the really curious part of the story is that at the very same moment, on all the other islands, all the other monkeys began to use it too — even though the islands were separated by many miles of sea, with no direct contact possible.

This phenomenon is seen as indicating that there is an evolutionary group consciousness that transcends normal sensory channels — at least as much in humans as in other primates. This clearly has enormous implications for our higher development, including at the planetary scale. Surely one of the most striking modern examples of the realisation of this potential must be the sudden, spontaneous outbreak, all over the civilised world at the same moment, of a completely new and ingenious way of making money: extorting it from captive drivers at slow traffic lights by unsolicitedly washing their windscreens.

Further reading:
The Hundredth Windscreen Washer by Walter J. Chrome — the story of one man's bid to get into the Guinness Book of Records by running people over at traffic lights.

I CHING

An ancient **oracle** or source of guidance which, with characteristic, inscrutably oriental sense of irony and paradox, is intended to actually *reduce* dependence on oracles. This is achieved by offering guidance which is so obscure that by the time the person consulting it has arrived at an understanding, the life situation about which they sought advice has completely altered, and so the reading is no longer relevant. To further enhance the effect, the language and metaphor derive from life in Imperial China around 4000 BC. For example:

PREPONDERANCE OF THE SMALL
When the three-toed cauldron sings yellow in the sunset,
The superior man will receive good fortune;
Beware the courtiers who bear dandelions
— It furthers one to walk backwards.

THROWING THE I CHING

IMMORTALISTS

A short-lived movement which was popular in California in the late '70s. Probably died out because it was so ageist, deathist and politically incorrect. The classic text is *How to Live for Ever*, by the late Hector Stiffkey.

INCARNATION

Transition from existence in the spirit realm, literally 'into a body' as a more-or-less human being. Spirits who wish to incarnate are said to buzz around, somewhat like flies or other insects, looking for two already-incarnated beings whom they consider suitable to 'come in' through. Individual humans who resist such conception can have a spirit buzzing round them for many years, until either an 'accident' happens or the spirit gives up or changes its mind.

Apparently, though, there is absolutely nothing accidental about the whole thing, and all three of the spirits eventually involved would have made a 'contract' together, possibly countless aeons ago, to 'manifest' at that particular time. Spirits probably get together wherever it is that they reside, and make a whole series of contracts for this particular eternity, rather like a very long series of dancing partners that people used to write on their sleeves at old-fashioned dances.

Spirits incarnate on Earth in order to progressively develop and grow as good little entities. According to Ram Dass, life with a human body is like a sort of schooling experience, where the curriculum is forward spiritual progress and cosmic evolution. Some spirits use a particular incarnation to get on with things and address issues still unresolved from past incarnations, while others spend the whole time hating school, being in detention, flunking exams, doing re-sits, repeating years and eventually 'dropping out'.

See also **Reincarnation**.

INNER CHILD

Inner refers to any part of ourselves which we want to let other people know needs attention, or wants sympathy or mollycoddling, as in "I'm working on my Inner Child." Other popular inner aspects are Inner Tyrant, Inner Wimp and Inner Pancreas.

INTEGRATIONAL STRUCTURING THROUGH PSYCHODYNAMIC COGNITIVE AWARENESS

Technical term for 'thinking'.

INTOLERANCE (or ALLERGY)

Perpetuation of childhood distastes into adult life. This is a very dangerous idea for children to get hold of, as in conversations such as this: "Eat up your greens." — "I don't like greens." — "How do you know you don't like greens? You've never tried them!" — "I know I don't like them. I've got a food intolerance to them."

Awareness of such reactions has been accepted in society for much longer than many suppose, as is shown in the original form of the old children's nursery rhyme:

Jack Spratt was allergic to fat;
His wife was intolerant of lean.
So they both became vegetarians
And thus licked their platters all clean.

You can, in fact, be allergic to almost anything — including New Age jargon.

JACUZZI

A technological approach to bathing that is rather older than most people imagine and which reflects two aspects of the era of its invention — the turbulence and communality of the French Revolution. The inventor was Jean Paul Marat, the radical polemicist, author and thinker. After successfully inciting the Sans-Culottes to revolt, Marat became accustomed to spending all his spare time in the bath, which he invariably shared with his mistress, Charlotte Corday. This was not only a direct result of the obligatory frequent attendances at close quarters to the guillotine, but also due to having to hide frequently in the sewers of Paris from his reactionary enemies. It is also well known that the bath was where he was fond of doing his writing.

The device itself acquired its name when the Sans-Culottes, suspecting that their one-time hero was becoming debauched by bourgeois tastes for luxury and hedonism, stormed his home. Finding him, as usual, reclining in the bath with his concubine, they set about attacking him with pumice stones and cottonbuds. But in the end it was the treacherous Charlotte who struck the fatal blow with a lavatory brush, to cries of "J'accuse! J'accuse!" And this name has stuck to the turbulent, communal bath experience ever since.

JUNG
See *Freud*.

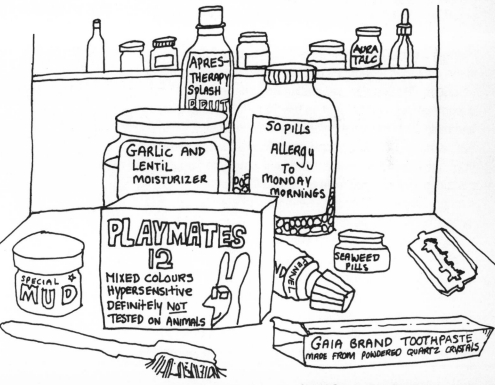

KARMA

Karma is an Eastern spiritual concept with no equivalent in Western materialist society, except in northern Yorkshire in England, where it is known as 'comeuppance'. Basically, the idea is that your deeds will always find you out, and you will always suffer the consequences of your actions, particularly as they affect other people. The good news, however, is that you can defer your karma forward in time, even into a future lifetime. This is known as accumulating 'Karmic Debt'. The bad news is that in such a future lifetime the consequences of your earlier action may affect you more disastrously, depending on your new circumstances, not to mention the 'Karmic Interest' that can build up if you leave it for too many lifetimes. Furthermore, very few people carry forward much memory from one lifetime to another, and so it is easy to forget the penalties that you may owe to people that have reincarnated in your circle. These people may then be forced to resort to the engagement of a 'Karmic Debt Collection Agency' for retribution, which is best avoided at all costs as these agencies are very unsympathetic, and have a minimum Karmic Call-Out Charge which they add to what you already owe. And they always get their man. Or their stone, if that's what you have reincarnated as.

Karma involves not only individuals but also groups of people, such as families — in which case all the individuals will invariably have extremely Heavy Negative Family Karma. The same applies to larger groups still, including countries themselves. When the Age of Aquarius finally arrives, Karmic Economics will be the main criterion for judging the health of a nation. All countries will be falling over themselves to genuinely help the others, in order to reduce their Karmic Deficit. Especially the USA.

KIRLIAN PHOTOGRAPHY

A form of intimate auric photography invented by the fin-de-siècle German erotic photographer Schorten Kirli.

KUNDALINI

The name of a famous Italian escapologist, and inventor of a method of moving one's sexual energy from the loins up to the crown of the head, though it is not known why this would be desirable. His notorious and fatal last escape using this method is said to have ended in terminal ecstasy.

LEY LINES

Patterns found on bedlinen after sexual activity.

LETS SCHEMES

Local Enterprise Schemes, or LETSs, are the leading edge of Green Economics, and are now sprouting up all over the UK. In Australia, USA and Canada (where the idea originated) they are now very highly developed, and exerting a positive influence on the conventional economic authorities.

LETS schemes are a refinement of old-fashioned bartering, but with the crucial addition of their own central banking and currency system. This means that each person trades with the system rather than directly with another individual. If you have too many free-range duck-eggs, for instance, and not enough fair-isle sweaters, you don't have to wait until you find someone with too many fair-isle sweaters and not enough free-range duck-eggs. You can just go to the person who has the sweaters and write a cheque for them in your local currency. These are 'Brights' if you are on the Brighton exchange, for example, and 'Strouds' in Stroud. In Totnes they call them 'Tots', and in Scarborough 'Scabs'. The citizens of Little Turdington have been unable to decide on a unit of currency.

So when other people buy duck-eggs, or whatever else you have to offer, they just give you a cheque, and all the cheques are sent in to central accounting. And the real beauty of the scheme is that you can have as much credit or overdraft as you want, and there is no interest payable or bank manager to breathe down your neck!

These schemes have only recently begun to attract any amount of attention, but they have in fact been on the go in obscure locations since back in the 1950s. All kinds of individuals have been waking up to their benefits — not least those with an interest in tax evasion.

The added attraction of becoming part of a different social structure, far from the eye of straight society, has appealed to yet another type of person — the one who has had too much attention from the public or who wants their secrets well-kept. It is a little-known fact that a considerable number of celebrities — even some who are thought to be dead — have, in fact, just 'dropped out', and perhaps come down a peg or two on the income scale, but nevertheless made a new life for themselves in just this kind of alternative situation. Here is a list of just some of the lesser-publicised examples, together with the location where they are now trading, and what they offer on their local exchange:

E. Presley (New Mexico): karaoke tuition

J. Hendrix (Portobello Road, London): guitar repairs

J. Joplin (Boulder, Colorado): voice workshops

B. Holly (Macchu Picchu): flying lessons

M. Bolan (Surbiton): dinosaur research services

M. Monroe (Beverly Hills): rolfing

R. Maxwell (Atlantis): ethical investment counselling

G. Garbo (Alice Springs): organising retreats

J. Dean (Avon Gorge): bungee jumping

I. Amin (Anchorage, Alaska): crystal healing

Q. Boadicea (Albion Retirement Home, Bournemouth): mechanical hedge trimming

M. Thatcher (Port Stanley, Falkland Islands): assertiveness training

N. Reagan (Washington DC): astrology charts

A. Hitler (Tierra del Fuego): step Reebok training

MACRONEUROTICS

An obscure food cult, which came from Japan in the 1950s and gained a considerable following among reformed drug dealers in the USA. Macroneurotics holds that food is the only important thing in the universe. The three main foods, held to be able to create total health, happiness, success, fulfilment and enlightenment, are brown rice with miso soup, brown rice with seaweed, and brown rice on its own.

The ultimate text is, of course, the Macroneurotic Bible; and the key passages are found in the Letters of St George O'Sawa to the Constipated. Chapter 7, Verses 1-29 contains the very core of Macroneurotics and its comparison with other 'paths':

Though I speak with the tongues of men and of angels, and have not Macroneurotics, I am become as a sounding bell or a tinkling cymbal.

For though I have the gift of prophecy and can do Tarot readings, and understand all earth mysteries and oracles, but have not Macroneurotics, then I am nothing.

And though I bestow all my goods to Oxfam or to the jumble sales of Guru Maharaji, and have not Macroneurotics, then it profiteth me nothing.

For I say unto you, Macroneurotics suffereth long, in fact is very much into suffering; Macroneurotics envieth not, and is not puffed up, unless by excessive consumption of rice cakes.

Macroneurotics never faileth. But whether there be vegetarians, they shall fail. And whether there be vegans, they shall be wrong too. And whether there be proponents of Food Combining, yeah verily, they shall all vanish away.

But when that which is perfect comes (ie brown rice), then that which is in part (white rice) shall be done away. For when I was a vegetarian, I spoke as a child; and when I became a vegan, I understood as a child; but when I became Macroneurotic, I put away childish things, and learned how to use chopsticks.

For now we see through a Cooking Class darkly, but then face to face. Now I know Macroneurotic Studies, but then shall I know Total World Domination.

And now abideth vegetarianism, veganism and Macroneurotics, these three; but the greatest of these is Macroneurotics.

MARRIAGE

Naturally, nobody gets married any more, but a number of alternatives have been available, and new ones are being thought of all the time. If you don't want to go for plain old cohabitation, or 'living in sin' in the old parlance, then you could try Handfasting. This is an ancient Celtic ritual where you get together each year and decide whether you both want to go on with it.

Alternatively, if all this still seems too much of a 'bind' as it were, you could go for one of the Californian-style marriage ceremonies, which can make an interesting

spontaneous diversion, especially outdoors on a picnic, or when a barbecue is going particularly well. You can just do whatever takes your fancy on the spur of the moment. Anyone, really, can take the part of the cleric, as long as they haven't had so much to drink that they can't stand up. Chartered accountants and civil servants are usually the easiest to talk into doing this job, but if you can book a druid in advance it will really add a lot more style.

See also **Relationship**, **Sex**.

M.E. DISEASE

Obsession with self.

MEDITATION

A popular and versatile method of suppressing uncomfortable emotions and ignoring unwelcome life events, or trying to get some value out of an activity that is otherwise a complete waste of time. There are many different types of meditation, including:

Sitting meditation
Walking meditation
Standing-at-a-bus-stop meditation
Giro-queue meditation
Driving-down-a-motorway meditation
Egg-boiling meditation
Escaping-from-having-to-do-the-washing-up meditation

MEDIUM

A medium is a person who **channels** an entity or phenomenon. The name has arisen because this activity, once rare and exciting, is now extremely commonplace, bland and nondescript (as in 'medium curry').

MEN'S WORK

Not an entirely New Age concept (as in "Stand back lass, this is men's work!"), but one that has certainly undergone a radical turnaround in recent years. Several turnarounds, in fact.

The first turnaround was the evolution of New Man (Homo Novo), now in fact extinct. New Man roamed the earth from about 1989 to about 1991 AD, and suffered from 'vagina envy'. New Man had noticed that New Woman, in fact all women, were very angry at him — indeed, were angry at all men. So he decided that the best thing to do was to agree with them, to admit that all men are Very Bad, to discover that he had Feelings, and to start being limp and pathetic instead of dominant and thrusting. But this made women even angrier. This is why New Man was an endangered species from the start.

The next turnaround came about directly from this. A big American poet named Bob Blythe, who was very angry at women over the extinction of New Man, wrote a book called *Stainless Steel John*, which is about the discovery of the Deep Masculine underneath the unwashed archetypal dishes at the bottom of the mythological kitchen sink. Modern man's problem with masculinity, Blythe said, was that he was deeply wounded by his father's consistent absence from the kitchen where the son was thus left perpetually in the clutches of his mom. The solution was to do a lot of ritualised barbecue initiations in the woods with a terrific amount of drumming, whooping and washing dishes in streams.

This movement too, however, soon lost momentum, mainly because Blythe's courses came to be filled with journalists doing features for the colour sections of newspapers, so that there was no room for regular guys. The movement that evolved in turn from this was naturally towards a more private, internalised and intimate experience of manhood, leading ultimately to the rediscovery of the penis. This phase reached its climax with the publication of Sam Keene's seminal book *Fire in the Willie*.

Things seemed, then, to be in the process of coming (sic) full circle, which they finally did when an anti-revisionist splinter group from this movement, going straight to the heart of what they saw as the *real* problem, took centre stage with a new battle-cry and began the 'Campaign for the Proper Woman'. This group just wanted everyone to catch themselves on, and return to the way things used to be, when you knew where you stood and said what you liked, and there wasn't any of this namby-pamby stuff like having feelings and thinking about things.

The diverse nature of the Men's Movement, then, has been a peculiarly circular phenomenon, which was also recognised by Andrew Dworkin in his ground-breaking 1993 essay 'Cross-Dressing in the Men's Movement'. Dworkin, however, suggested a different breakdown or categorisation of the movement, and identified five sub-movements, with each branch typified by its position in relation to anger. There have been, he argued, the 'We're really angry' men; the 'Let's look at our anger' men; the 'It isn't OK to be angry' men, the 'Let's try to get angry' men; and the 'What's this anger thing everybody's on about?' men. Each of these groups, Dworkin said, was angry at most of the others, and women were extremely angry at them all.

MISTAKE

There isn't any such thing nowadays — there are only 'learning experiences'.

MONEY

Money in the New Age, apparently, is nothing special — it's just another form of *energy*. Some people, unfortunately, never seem to have much *energy*.

MOTHER STUFF

Stuff about your mother. Mother stuff is at the bottom of all psychological, emotional and therapeutic problems. See also *Anger*.

MOUNTAIN BIKE

An oddly named vehicle, which in point of fact is almost exclusively found on flat terrain in urban areas. Perhaps for this reason it is more correctly known as the ATB (or Around Town Bike).

The vehicle is actually more frequently employed as a posing aid than as a mode of transport, and is usually observed either permanently attached to a lamp-post with saddle, front wheel and handlebars missing, or accompanied by a static non-cyclist clad in lurid skin-tight lycra-wear.

Prized features of the ATB are: instantly obsolescent technological innovations, myriad specialised and useless accessories, and aggressive brand names. Cognoscenti opine that the true origin of the misnomer 'mountain' actually lies in its steepness of price.

MUSIC

Everyone knows about the burgeoning market in so-called New Age Music, that bland blend of synth and slush that one hears everywhere now from seance to supermarket. But the music that really has got something substantial to give to heightening of consciousness is, in fact, Country and Western. C&W, people are now beginning to realise, is more than just a type of music; it is a whole *therapy* in itself.

C&W has long been a vehicle for powerful emotion and issues around relationship, but for various reasons this feature has until recently been regarded as somehow shameful and stigmatic. Now, however, the full therapeutic value of this musical form is coming to be recognised. C&W has at last begun to blossom in the deep, fertile soil of the field of personal development, and is no longer regarded as the ugly, despicable weed it was once considered.

The subject-matter of C&W is in a very real sense the neglected material of the New Age Movement. That whole cult has become completely obsessed with spreading love and light and thinking happy thoughts — it's all about 'accentuate the positive, forget about the negative, and go forward into the New Era with shining aura and effervescent chakras'. But the true sages have always known that we must face up to the other side of the coin as well — and this is what Country and Western does. It embraces the Shadow; it recognises old and deeply-suppressed pain, tragedy, grief, shame and loss; it gives full rein to co-dependency, low self-esteem, self-sacrifice and sheer self-perpetuating gloom. And it uses all the standard tools of personal growth towards these noble ends: affirmations, self-reflection, dialogue, visualisation and comprehensive image-work, to name but a few — and all in refreshingly *negative* ways.

Guilt, denial, hatred and the unconscious death-wish — none of these usually taboo subjects is shied away from in C&W. Titles like 'Every night I cry myself to sleep', 'This world ain't my home', or 'I'll be happy when I'm six feet down' will always be psychotherapeutic standards. 'Heartache is my friend'; 'She left me for a down-and-out'; 'I've loved and lost a thousand times'; these too are Therapy-of-the-Dark-Side classics. 'Failure is what I do best', too — it's all powerful, healing stuff. It easily surpasses the Blues, or even the Celtic Dirge.

But the latest 'New Country' music goes a step further still, explicitly recognising and acknowledging the burden of debt that society owes to the much-maligned genre, and openly drawing on the language of transformation and *growth*. And growth *is* the word — this is fast becoming financially the biggest growth area in mainstream popular music. Concepts no one heard of a few years ago are now the catch-lines in million-sellers. People are going to C&W concerts instead of signing up for life-changing workshops. They are getting therapy through seeing the singing stars on their TV sets. Titles like 'Crying into my camomile tea', 'Rescue Remedy under my pillow', and 'Born under a lonesome sign' — these are the new classics. And more poignant still: 'Why does your Analyst always let you down?' Or facing up to that worst scenario of all: 'My wife's run off with my Counsellor (an' I'm missin' him so bad)'.

NAM-MYO-HO-RENGE-KYO

A popular form of *chanting*, the constant repetition of which is very helpful in achieving goals in life, particularly finding a parking space. Chanting is a way of exploring our metaphysical relationship with the cosmos, figuring as a kind of archetypal parent figure. As archetypal children who want things, we quickly learn that if we keep repeating something over and over again, sooner or later the universe will give in and let us have our way, just for a bit of peace and quiet. Other useful chants: Om-mane-padme-hum; Hare-krishna/hare-krishna/krishna-krishna/hare-hare; Gimme-gimme-gimme etc.

NDE

An extreme form of indecisiveness, the Near Death Experience, is dying and then changing your mind and coming back to life again. Once extremely rare, it is now extremely commonplace; no one in New Age circles is anyone unless they have had at least one NDE. Characteristic features reported with this ploy include experiencing a deep feeling of peace and tranquillity; leaving your body in a hospital bed or on an operating table and hovering up near the ceiling, while wondering what all the fuss and panic among the nurses and doctors below you is all about; travelling down a long, dark tunnel towards a beautiful, clear light; hearing divine sounds from choirs of heavenly angels; and getting tangled up in the silver cord that still connects you to your body — unless you finally decide you're not going back (in which case it's a DE rather than an NDE). Much more rare these days is the NLE, or Near Life Experience.

NEGATIVE

Not *positive*. The word negative is currently not in vogue, and in fact it has been getting something of a raw deal for quite some time, mainly due to the current sinister and systematic programme of positive brainwashing. Clearly there is nothing 'better' or 'worse' about negativity; in time to come, no doubt, the pendulum will swing the other way, and positivity will be just as arbitrarily 'not okay'. Besides, it is widely acknowledged that people who are into Positivity are seen as superior, snobbish and 'holisticker than thou'*. Negativity, on the other hand, is great for working on the Shadow or darker side of our nature, which of course Positivity freaks prefer to believe does not exist. And it's just more downright *realistic*.

See also *Music*.

* In yoga circles, a 'pain in the asana'.

NEGATIVE AFFIRMATIONS
Many books and teachers of *affirmations* do not even acknowledge the possibility of any other kind than positive;

in point of fact, many of the very finest affirmations are negative ones. There's a lot to be said for NAs: they are easier to think of, easier to put into practice, and they come to most of us a lot more easily. Traditional speech, indeed, displays a strong tendency to NAs. "Life isn't a bed of roses, you know"; "Money doesn't grow on trees"; "You can't be too careful these days." Even our vernacular responses to greetings tend to be inspired by the same solid, grounded, down-to-earth influence: "Good Morning, and how are you today?" "Oh, you know, struggling . . ." Or "Mustn't grumble." Roughly translated, these responses mean "Okay, thank you." Or if someone is *really* feeling rather good, it's "So-so", "Could be worse" or "Fair-to-middling".

But the greatest source of inspiration for the serious student of Negative Affirmations lies in common underlying societal attitudes to the basic processes of life. Tradition here too supplies some stalwart approaches. How many of us have been brought up to believe that really welcome events are bound to be 'too good to be true'; that 'it's good to feel down because then you can only go up'; that 'the higher you climb the harder you fall; and just generally not to expect too much from life because then you won't be disappointed. After all, 'things often have to get worse before they get better'. So be realistic, expect worse *still*. And remember, money doesn't grow on trees. It is on such sturdy fare that the great Negative Affirmers of our time have been raised. Here, then, are a few more personal NAs that can form the basis of a really good repertoire:

"Life is a struggle."
"There's never enough of anything."
"There's something terribly wrong with me."
"Nobody loves me."
"I have to do everything for myself."
"I'm a totally helpless victim of fate."
"Everyone wants to hurt me."
"It's all my fault."
"I am truly paranoid (ask any of my friends)."

But if you do inadvertently slip up and find yourself making an ambitious and positive request from the universe, you can always qualify it with a little negative rider such as '—sometime soon perhaps', '— if it isn't too much trouble', or even '— or if things can't get better, could I have them just getting worse more slowly?'

NETWORKING

Networkers are people who are terminally restless and can't decide where to settle down and what to do with themselves. They are incredibly secretive about themselves, but enjoy meddling in other people's affairs, and would probably be tabloid gossip columnists if they weren't in the New Age Movement. They are usually born under the sign of Aquarius.

PEN

A highly desirable state these days; apparently everyone should be open all the time. It is much better to be open than closed, shut, impermeable or impenetrable. No one really knows why.

ORACLES

Systems of divination, such as *I Ching*, Tarot or Low-Caffeine Tealeaf Readings. See also *Astrology*.

ORGANIC GROWING

Organic Growing used to simply mean 'growing things organically'. Unfortunately the reputation of OG has suffered lately owing to the increasing practice by commercial middlemen who buy up large stocks of regular factory-farmed produce, add artificial worm-holes and other blemishes, knock the stuff about a bit to cause bruising, and mix up different sizes to simulate the authentic organic look, which discerning shoppers are now known to seek. They then sell it to the supermarkets at a huge mark-up.

OUT-OF-BODY

Having an out-of-body experience or OOB is rather like going to a kind of cosmic nudist camp, where it is thought perfectly natural, and even healthier, to go about without a body. You just sort of check it in before you enter the camp, and collect it again as you leave, in order to re-enter so-called normal reality. Actually, from the overall spiritual perspective of existence, having a body or 'incarnation' is only a phase we pass through. For most of the countless aeons that our spirits exist, we probably don't have one; so an OOB experience is most likely just a temporary revisiting of this state for refreshment and renewal. There are quite a lot of fun things you can do with a body, though, it must be admitted.

PARENTING

A pretentious and jargonistic term for 'having children'.
(See also *Family*)

PAST LIVES

The concept of past lives could well have been invented by
people who don't want to deal with their present difficulties,
and then perpetuated by others who soon realised that it
would be a great ruse to earn a lot of money, by offering
Past Life Regression and other expensive services.

Interestingly enough, those who 'remember' past lives
only recall previous *incarnations* as people who were
incredibly prominent, powerful and exotic — great kings
and queens, brave warriors, barbaric rulers, celebrated
concubines or other ancient celebrities. No one ever has a
past life as an ancient Egyptian janitor or an Imperial
Roman dishwasher. Such people, apparently, do not
reincarnate (qv).

A lot of people have difficulty believing in past lives.
Freud, for instance, unlike *Jung*, thought that believing in
past lives and reincarnation was merely a way of avoiding
having to accept one's own mortality, which would
otherwise cause us to blame our mother for bringing us
into the world, which would in turn compromise our intense
hatred for our father. But then of course, as Adler would
point out, that was Freud's *karma*. Freud, he commented,
"didn't believe in past lives in his other incarnations,
either."

PATTERN

A repetitive sequence of experiences or behavioural traits that are not necessarily significant in themselves, but have the effect of annoying other people more than the person to whom the pattern belongs. In fact, one of the most virulent forms of pattern is that of being annoyed by other people's patterns.

PATTERNOMETER: electronic device for detecting when you are getting into a *pattern*.

PAVLOV

Inventor of a radical form of therapy which uses a dessert made from rich meringues with lashings of cream, to cure people who think they are dogs.

PEAK EXPERIENCE

The zenith or climactic point in a series of subjective events.

Much sought-after in modern, goal-orientated materialistic society, the peak experience is inherently flawed and can never fulfil its promise of superlative reward or pleasure. The drawback with the peak experience is that, by definition, it is impossible for you as experiencer to tell whether what you are experiencing is the actual peak of the experience, or whether there is something better to come, until the experience has definitely gone into decline, by which time the opportunity to savour the PE is lost for ever.

Identical twins who are in separate locations and receive this phenomenon by psychic link are in fact having a Twin Peak Experience. This is even less satisfactory.

PETS

Pets have always been popular, but the trend in pets these days is much more towards more interesting and spiritually uplifting pets, such as whales and dolphins, praying mantises, or **angels**, devas and fairies. The conscious pet-owner today is also interested in teaching pets to do interesting things, such as **meditate**, give you **therapy** or **channel** an entity.

See also pets as **Relationship Role Models**.

PET THERAPY

Alternative health practices for the treatment of pets is another huge growth field, with constant opportunity for fresh ideas, and all the more so because of the exotic

my Life hasn't been the same since I did that 'NEW AGE Knitting patterns from Atlantis' WORKSHOP!

factor in pet choice itself. Homoeopathy for dogs and cats, or acupuncture for farm animals is old hat; now it's Alexander Method for snakes, Feldenkrais for gerbils and Dynamic Integration for sloths.

But perhaps the most radical departure in recent times is actually training the animals themselves to give the treatment to their owners. The training process can be a risky business, but the rewards can be great; we will soon be able to avail ourselves of porcupine acupuncture, rolfing by elephant and possibly even skunk aromatherapy.

PHYSICS, THE NEW

Fritjof Capra, in his book *The Tao of Physics*, introduced ordinary New Age people to the wonderful world of the new physics — quarks, neutrons, protons and mysterons; strings and superstrings, gluons and supergluons — with its whole new jargon, the eloquent language of a Cosmic Dance, words such as 'charm', 'strangeness' and 'sex appeal'. At the same time, he pointed out the radical 'new' concepts of physics — the interconnectedness of everything (or the recognition that there isn't really any difference between 'matter' and 'energy'); that what's going on in the universe is actually affected by how we observe it (or that the underlying only real thing that ultimately exists is in fact 'consciousness'. And he pointed out that these concepts are not so new at all, but have in fact been present in the cosmology of ancient thinkers such as

Taoists and Buddhists all along. The ordinary Tibetan monk in the ordinary Tibetan monastery in ordinary Tibet in the early middle ages would have been perfectly aware of these concepts, albeit expressed in his own terms (Tibetan). Capra is said to have made this important realisation while listening to the original radio broadcast of 'The Hitch-Hiker's Guide to the Galaxy'.

Stephen Hawkings, too, in his magnum opus *A Short History of Life, the Universe and Everything*, introduced an even wider universe to the transparent simplicity and sheer elementariness of advanced particle physics. As a result of this trend, the work of many great physicists of the past is being re-examined, and many formerly discredited names are being rehabilitated as their little-known work on the application of esoteric physics to ordinary aspects of every-day life is uncovered. We all know that Newton thought a lot about apples, for instance, but what we didn't know about until recently was Einstein's special interest in food.

EINSTEIN'S LAWS OF TOAST

It is fairly well known that Albert Einstein's most brilliant thoughts came to him not in the lab but when he was at leisure — out in the garden, perhaps, or in his favourite rocking-chair, or maybe even on the toilet. What is not so well known is that his real source of inspiration was the kitchen. And what hardly anyone knows is that his most penetrating insights came through working with toast.

Einstein was in fact much more preoccupied with the mundane physics of everyday life than with the rarefied world of experimental research and higher mathematics. The interaction of people with matter was what interested him most of all.

At a very early age Albert perceived what a vital role toast could play in the drama of family life. On many occasions his father abandoned the family in their small Swiss chalet on the grounds of unsatisfactory toast. Little Albert swore then that he would dedicate his life to discovering the secret of this substance, which seemed to have the power to hold the family together or break it apart.

Einstein's empirical research into toast, in fact, dwarfs the significance of his more celebrated efforts; to him, toast represented the perfect model for the workings of the universe. By 1885, at the tender age of six, Albert was already a prodigy in the field of burnt-particle physics, purely from observations of his parents' mistakes. The following year he began his own secret experiments at home, every time the rest of the family went out for a picnic.

After some years of intense, snatched studies, he began to get somewhere. Little though he realised it at the time, he was actually beginning to understand the very behaviour of matter. Through a mixture of pragmatism and intuition he was on the verge of discovering, at the tender age of nine, what mainstream quantum physics was not to clarify until the 1960s and 1970s — that the behaviour of matter and energy is actually altered by our interaction with it.

Toast was indeed the perfect medium for investigating this concept. After more years of surreptitious research, in the late spring of 1905, young Einstein was ready to announce to the world his Special Theory of Toast. He did not reveal it, however, to the scientific establishment, but in the obscure Swiss *Chemistry-Set User's Gazette*, thus avoiding the publicity that his 'official' work was by now attracting.

The Special Theory or First Law of Toast is a beguilingly simple expression of the physics of relativity, and part of its appeal is undoubtedly its quaint, vernacular language. "If you are making toast," the theory states, "and you ask if anyone else would like some, and they say no; then if you make only enough for yourself, they will change their minds and there won't be enough."

These words would not shake the world as did Einstein's more famous hypothesis, but their impact inevitably percolated into the rarefied strata of academia. So it was that, the very next year, Einstein was offered directorship of the prestigious Academy of Domestic Science in Berlin. Here he would continue his beloved studies, no longer hampered by lack of funds, inferior apparatus or having to do the washing up.

This should have been the happiest of times for Albert, but he was haunted by many still unanswered questions. Ironically, he was so far ahead of the thinking of his time that he alone could see how much further there was to go. For ten years he strove to resolve the shortcomings of his first theory, and at last achieved the breakthrough; in 1915, with war raging unnoticed in the outside world, he triumphantly published his General Theory of Toast. Again it was in a less-than-avant-garde organ — the Berlin *Train Spotter's Weekly*. And again it went largely unnoticed.

The General Theory or Second Law of Toast went a lot further than its predecessor. "If you are making toast", it stated, "and you ask the others if they want some and they say no; and you think, 'Well, I'm sure they'll change their minds,' so you make some extra; then they won't and you'll have too much toast."

After this Einstein sensed that there wasn't much further to go in this direction, and switched the emphasis of his work to isolating the active element in burnt toast that could unleash such devastating forces in the home. In 1920 he achieved this, using controlled nuclear fission in an Aga solid-fuel cooking range; the newly-isolated element would be posthumously named after him. But by now it was becoming impossible to keep any part of his studies private, and in 1921 he was obliged to accept the Nobel Peace Prize in recognition of the value of his work to world peace through increased domestic harmony. By the 1930s his name was a household word.

However, life was no bed of roses for a highly unorthodox Jewish thinker in post-war Nazi Germany, and in 1933 Albert was persuaded to move to the USA. Joining the elite Institute of Advanced Culinary Studies at MIT, he experienced a new surge of creativity. Here at last his profound understanding of the interrelationship of time, mass and velocity blossomed in his invention of the pop-up toaster.

This was the last high point of Einstein's career; after it came only despair and disillusion. He spent many years endeavouring to incorporate gravity into his theories, but the discovery of a formula that would explain why buttered toast always falls the wrong way up consistently eluded him. Likewise, for all his profound understanding of relativity, he never solved the paradox of the behaviour of toast that doesn't cook at all when you are standing over it, but burns as soon as you move away. More heartbreaking still, he spent the last years of his academic career fruitlessly seeking the long-awaited 'Unified Field Theory' in the under-researched area of making toast out of doors.

The scientific establishment has never been able to admit that this was the arena where Einstein did his most important thinking. Consequently, the full impact of his work still has not been absorbed. If only this man had allowed the world to know more of his activities and the latent potential to create harmony, then perhaps his findings would not have resulted in the capacity to destroy the planet.

This abuse drove Einstein into a self-imposed exile of total silence. He swore that he would reveal no more theories, and we can only guess at what these might have been. But we do know that he considered toast to be the basic material that holds our universe together; and modern physicists tacitly admit that his work with burnt toast particles led to his discovery of the existence of Black Holes as early as 1951.*

In 1955, Albert Einstein — thinker, pacifist, Jew and amateur breakfast chef — died. To the end he maintained that it will only be a matter of time before humankind discovers, in a nearby galaxy, a dark, cold planet composed entirely of burnt toast.

* Stephen Hawkings: *A Brief History of Toast,* pub. Big-Breakfast Books.

POSITIVE

Not *negative* (qv). See *Affirmations*.

PMT

Pre-menstrual tension. More aware individuals, especially male partners of sufferers of PMT, have recently recognised that the conventional explanation of it is an unacceptably sexist, simplistic and inadequate description of the phenomenon. Experts now agree on a broad outline for an alternative and more far-reaching analysis of this mood-altering female cycle. PMT does not actually occur in isolation; it is nearly always preceded by pre-PMT, and usually succeeded by post-PMT, which in turn is followed by MT, or simple menstrual tension. Sometimes there is a brief delay before the cycle recommences with pre-PMT, but this is acknowledged as increasingly rare. See also *stress*.

POST-

Prefix designed to give the impression that societal progress is being made when it probably isn't, as in Post-Feminism, Post-Constructivism and Postal Delays.

POST-FREUDIAN TENSION

Anxiety following a spell of psychoanalysis.

POST-NATAL DEPRESSION

PMT researchers (see above) have discovered a remarkable similarity of patterns in the area of depression. That is to say, Post-Natal Depression is usually preceded by a brief bout of Natal Depression, which typically follows a spell of Pre-Natal Depression. The whole cycle was once thought to last only for one lifetime, but reincarnation experts are currently looking into the possibility of the existence of Past Life Depression. ('Bad *karma*, man')

POST-NATAL-CHART DEPRESSION

Depression that results from reading a particularly truthful and hard-hitting astrology chart.

POWER POINT

A kind of 'socket' on the earth's own 'electrical wiring system', where 'aware' individuals can go to 'plug in' to the 'energy supply'. Sedona, Arizona has three of these in its vicinity, and the Tibetan Himalayas are full of them, which is why China is so keen to stay in there.

PROPER JOB

Term of abuse popular with mothers of alternative health practitioners, or of people who are taking time to sort out their *stuff*, and of those on any kind of spiritual path — as in, "Why don't you get a proper job?" (See also *Mother Stuff*)

PRIMAL INTEGRATION

A very funny therapy — in fact, it's quite a scream.

PROSPERITY

Abundance, wealth or plentifulness. After *relationship*, this is the second most popular subject for *affirmations, visualisation* and *chanting.* However, like relationship, it is a highly paradoxical phenomenon: the people who rely on these methods to achieve prosperity seem to be the ones whom it most effectively eludes. (See *Rebirthing*.)

PROTECTION

1. Creating an aura of visualised white light around your house or car so that you don't get broken into, towed away or clamped. Unfortunately, evolved burglars and traffic wardens in 'aware' cities nowadays are beginning to carry powerful and advanced white-light dispersing equipment .

2. If you are a healer, enclosing yourself in a visualised golden bubble when you are trying to heal someone who isn't very nice.

ASTRAL PROTECTION
Wearing an etheric condom during astral sex.

PSYCHIC

A psychic is a person who is intuitive and able to pick up on information from subtle and intangible sources. The word is actually a degeneration of 'sidekick'; the first known 'psychic' was in fact Tonto, the Lone Ranger's trusty companion, who never failed to track down villains by instinctive means, and always noticed things that the masked lawman didn't.

PSYCHODRAMA

A form of therapy which involves a lot of fuss and bother, as in 'making a psychodrama out of a crisis'.

PURPLE PLATES

Specially coloured crockery which effectively neutralises any *negative energy* that may have occurred due to use of non-organic ingredients, or watching a violent movie while cooking, or being in the middle of a family squabble while eating.

REBIRTHING

Most rebirthers these days do not admit that this is what they do; they have another therapy that they use as a front. This is partly because rebirthing can be an extremely messy business and partly because being born was horrible and most people want to forget it. It is a fairly reliable sign that you may be in for an unsolicited rebirthing experience if you hear your therapist calling for "Plenty of hot water!"

For some reason, rebirthers have developed a distinctive style of speech, which probably represents the pinnacle of infuriating New Age jargon (see also **Communication**). Some of their favourite expressions include: "What's coming up for you right now?", "How did you manage to create that experience?" and "It's all part of your process."

RECYCLING

Gathering up all kinds of waste products in the home — bottles, cans, plastics, newspapers, lentils, toenail clippings, nappies etc; then carefully sorting them into their respective categories; and keeping them for several months in your hallway or under the stairs, until they are finally thrown away in despair with the rest of the regular rubbish.

RECOVERY

Probably the fastest-developing area of the personal growth movement, which has evolved out of the famous 'Twelve Steps' approach to recovery from addiction to alcohol and other substance abuse. These principles have been systematically applied to more and more areas of human dependence, from addiction to destructive relationships to having an unbreakable **pattern** of trying to solve every problem by making a nice cup of tea.

But perhaps the most significant sector of the modern Recovery From Dependency movement — and the most fiercely competitive — is roadside recovery. And the most radical recent entry to this lucrative marketplace must be Astral Auto, the new holistic motorists' roadside help service that is sweeping the competition off the highways. It sports a number of revolutionary services to breakdown sufferers that are unmatched by competitors: instant onward astral travel for driver and up to four passengers to planned destination, with vehicle to follow by conventional means; free **Bach Flower Rescue Remedy** (qv) supplied immediately to counteract the bad vibrations and general shock of breakdown; and hot organic vegetarian soup carried by all operatives, or tofu ice cream in summer.

REINCARNATION

Reappearance of a spirit on Earth, complete with body, mind, soul and usually very poor memory (see also

Incarnation). We have learned a great deal about the subject since the advent of reincarnation therapists, who use regression and inform everyone that they are Old Souls, ie they have reincarnated many, many times, which is thought to be much better than not having reincarnated many, many times. People are now beginning to realise that having reincarnated many times is rather like having had sex with a lot of different people, in that a) it is something you can boast about, but b) people might not want to be in relationship with you because of it. Apparently there aren't any Young Souls about, or Middle-Aged Souls for that matter, or if there are, then they don't go to see reincarnation therapists.

One possible explanation that has been put forward for the shortage of Young Souls these days is to do with moral fibre. The entry requirements for New Souls are thought to be extremely demanding. In times long past, entities were made of sterner stuff, and were prepared to undergo the untold aeons of preparatory work. The apprentices of today just don't have the attention span for the job.

See also *Past Lives*, *Karma*.

REINCARNATION AGENCIES

Reincarnation professionals are near to setting up commercial operations which will offer a wide range of personal services related to reincarnation — especially finding out about past lives and making choices about future ones. They plan to feature products such as Past Life CVs, Future Life Indemnity Insurance, Archival Research on prospective partners, really Long-Term Job Applications, discharge of Karmic Debts and Next-Time-Round Cosmic Dating services. People will be able to get together with that rather special someone, but in circumstances that they would prefer — eg with each person changed to the other sex — or they may wish to arrange some very elaborate measures for future revenge, or even bequeath themselves a nice little nest-egg in times to come.

Believers in Reincarnational Determinism (the concept that it has all been worked out long ago and therefore can't be altered) will not be eligible for any of these services.

Government sources admit that they are unofficially very disquieted by these proposals because of the possibilities of almost undetectable abuse of the system, including major fraud and tax evasion. They are very unsure whether it will be possible to legislate, for instance, against people who die so that their relatives receive compensation from life insurance, and then reincarnate straight away as a new member of the same family.

RELATIONSHIP

A temporary conjunction between two spiritual entities, currently manifesting as human beings, in order to *grow* through experiencing difficulties.

Research has shown that 91% of all *affirmations* and wishes for improvement are concerned with love relationships. 57% are made with the intention of creating 'a wonderful, fulfilling, satisfying, intimate relationship'. 24% are hoping for 'a better relationship than the one I am in at the moment'. 11% are seeking 'any relationship at all', and 22% wish they 'could get out of their current relationship'.

It is generally accepted that the purpose of the sexual urge is for the species to maintain itself. The reason we have relationships, on the other hand, is to have our buttons pushed, to find out what our unresolved stuff is about, and to get things about ourselves dragged into the open, which we have been spending our lives hiding from other people.

There are many different ways of approaching relationships and how to have better ones. A number of different methods of analysis and approaches to improvement are dealt with here.

MODELS FOR RELATIONSHIP

Dogs have very simple needs and wants: they want their food; they want to go out and run about a lot — back and forward, round in circles and after sticks; and they want to have company, preferably with their owner, whom they like a lot, and quite unconditionally. As long as they get these things, they are usually completely happy. They don't say to themselves, "Oh that wasn't what I wanted after all, this other thing was what I wanted; what I want now is something completely different." They don't keep 'moving the goalposts' all the time. Dogs are excellent models for

being in a relationship; in fact the reason why dogs manifested on the planet was to aid human beings as relationship role models, and they decided that the best way to do this would be to let humankind think that they were 'domesticating' them. Unfortunately, very few humans realise that this is why dogs spend time with them, and even fewer manage to apply the lessons in their relationships.

Cats, by contrast, are independent, contrary, changeable, demanding and unpredictable. Cats realised that dogs had pretty much sewn up the straightforward/ dependable/know-where-you-are-with-them relationship stuff, so they would do something completely different. In fact, they decided that they would portray how *not* to be in a relationship. If cats aren't made a fuss of every hour or so, they will quite readily call the whole relationship off — at least until the next time they are hungry. And if they want to make a point, they will only eat the most expensive cat food. If it's a major point, they'll go off their food altogether. Sad to say, humanity got the whole thing completely the wrong way round, and have been emulating cats rather than dogs in their relationships ever since. But then that's one of the dangers when you are the dominant species *and* have free will.

Early on in their evolution, gerbils decided that there must be something that they too could do to help humans out of the difficulties inherent in being a more highly sophisticated and versatile species. What they came up with was the ultimate how-not-to model for relationship contentment — being totally happy to run round and round all day in a little wheel. Unfortunately the point has once more been missed by the bulk of humanity, so there are a great many people who go for the running-round-and-round-in-a-wheel-all-day, not-particularly-going-anywhere kind of relationship, and the gerbil is probably a great inspiration to them all.

The origin of every human way-of-being-in-relationship, in fact, has derived from a pattern set by one of the many animal species that have chosen the karmic path of proximity to man. Those people, for instance, who are terribly aware of difficulties in relationship, put a lot of effort into creating difficulties in relationship, and are unable to operate in any other context than that of difficulties in relationship, are probably prone to the influence of the broody hen, with perhaps a touch of the sick parrot.

Those other people, on the other hand, who really do not like difficulties, are not prepared to deal with difficulties, and in fact refuse to admit that difficulties even exist, are probably more inspired by ostriches, and it is interesting to note how popular ostrich farms are becoming these days, far from the creature's homeland. Those who only want a relationship with themselves are really worm types, and probably are likewise working as hard as they can to evolve and develop the organs of both sexes. But comprehensive irritability in relationship is the special dispensation of the goat.

Other creatures that are specially influential as relationship role models: budgies, terrapins, boa constrictors, snapping turtles, sheep, stick insects, and the ever-popular goldfish.

RESCUE REMEDY

A **Bach Flower Remedy** for treating shock, injury, trauma, **stress** or indeed anything happening that you don't particularly like. Addiction to Rescue Remedy is statistically the most prevalent substance abuse among sensitive, aware, New Age people.

See also **Recovery**.

RETREAT

A confusing term for activities such as **meditation** which, paradoxically, are actually meant to be concerned with spiritual advance.

ROLFING

An extremely vigorous and painful form of bodywork practised by people who have invariably had **past lives** in the Spanish Inquisition, and who are having a go at doing something more constructive this time around.

SAMYE LING

Celebrated Scottish Buddhist teacher who was very fond of fish.

SEX

In the post-chauvinist, post-feminist, post-modernist era, the art of sexual negotiation is a whole new ball-game, so to speak. It isn't the minefield it once was, with the ever-present danger of instant accusation of sexism after some minor slip-up in etiquette; nor is being totally 'cool' the strict requirement it once was. Nevertheless rules are rules, and the risk of making a gaffe is as great — if not greater — than ever. Only the penalties have changed. In this day and age, under-arm hair may be perfectly acceptable, even compulsory; but one still runs the risk of appearing unreconstructed, unevolved, unenlightened or, worse still, full of unresolved stuff about one's mother. So carefully chosen opening lines are all the more vital. And first impressions last.

If you are in the organic greengrocer, for instance, and you have just seen someone you think that you might like more than yourself, you could lead in with something simple like: "Excuse me, but I couldn't help noticing how clear your aura is", or "Do you manifest here often?"

For something a little more audacious — perhaps while hanging out at the vegetarian barbecue or the smoke-free, lager-free, leather-free disco: "Hi, I'm Tarquin and I notice you're really comfortable in your body" may evoke a favourable response. For the more suppressed individual, "Do you know, the 'I Ching' said I would meet someone just like you today" might be a better bet. Having broken the ice, your intuition may guide you to be a little more adventurous: "Gosh, you really remind me of my last soul-mate!" Or, if you're prone to use of flattery, you could slip in "Oh wow, what a coincidence — I'm in my last incarnation too!" Never mind about implausibility — you get extra points for ingenuity here. Remember, just like in the Real World, it's still all just a game: the oldest game in the world.

Later on, you might think that *you* might be comfortable in their body too, so why not try for a date? Something innocent, yet with potential for intimacy, is always a good bet here. "Would you like to be my partner at the drop-in Shiatsu class on Friday evening?" is often well received, and implies that you already know how to do a mean piece of bodywork, which is always an added incentive. "Fancy a sweat in my authentic two-person Native American Sweatlodge?" is good too. Or if they do already seem interested: "How about swapping some 'Intimate Touch' treatment this weekend?" (Or ". . . this evening?" Or ". . . right now?") On the other hand, proposing that you attend the Hands-On Tantric Sex workshop as a couple lacks subtlety. You have to play the game.

Of course, following the correct protocol for being on the other end and replying to such solicitations is important too. Whatever way the lead-in is formulated, don't just say, "Okay, what time?" Take the opportunity to really enter into the spirit of the quest for personal growth, spiritual adventure — and probably sex. Something like "Your suggestion has set my heart chakra all aglow with a raging fire of eager anticipation", sounds perhaps a shade too keen; a simple "This feels very right" or "I'm getting a definite 'yes' from my Higher Self" is quite sufficient.

Proper forms for declining such invitations are equally relevant, and cover everything from gentle discouragement to firm rebuttal. Having an authoritative excuse which will be acceptable to the inviter is always a good way of avoiding offence, so you don't have to say something like "No way, I wouldn't mingle energies with you if the future of the planet depended on it." Far better to go for one of the safe standard replies: "Sorry, I can't do Saturday, I'm having an out-of-body experience/doing some astral projection/staying at home to cleanse my aura." Or perhaps "Not just at the moment — I've got to work on my relationship affirmations/just be with myself for a while/do a colonic irrigation" (always a good one for putting people off).

But let's assume instead that your energies do turn out to be harmonious; you go out on the date, and you both have a really meaningful, fulfilling and mutually growthful evening. Then follows the all-important moment — do you both go your separate ways home, or is there something else on the cosmic agenda? In this time-honoured scenario, "Would you like to come up for a Tarot reading/for a cup of camomile tea/to see my Kirlian photography?" is always a safe format, which also offers a range of let-out options that aren't too personally down-putting to the asker (viz. "I'd love to, but I'm allergic to camomile/I disapprove of unsolicited readings/I've an ecological objection to the chemicals used in Kirlian photography"). If the solicitee *does* prove resistant, and *you* are still as keen as ever, it's worth trying ". . . but my Karmic Counsellor says our destinies are inextricably intertwined!"

Finally, you do manage to get upstairs with the candidate. You are both listening to your new whalesong CD; it only remains to touch on the subject of sex. You both clearly want to *do* it; all that's necessary is to bring it into the open a bit. Going on about 'some good methods you know for releasing deep-seated tension' are a bit old-hat these days, but you can always try the angle that 'their base chakra energy seems somewhat stuck and maybe you could help them move it a bit'. And if any question of guilt arises, it can be reassuring to remember that you are not really being promiscuous; you're just 'working through some stuff'/'being true to your spontaneous feelings'/ 'learning how to Really Let Go'.

In the last analysis, though, a touch of humour at this juncture is probably your best strategy in overcoming nervousness and embarrassment. *Everyone* likes to be laughed into bed. This approach can also help if anything laughable happens — or *fails* to happen — later on. A cheeky little starter to have up your sleeve might be something like, "You know, I'm convinced that we were married to each other in a past life, but due to a personal tragedy the marriage was never consummated. Mind you, it may not be too late to do something about it now . . ." Some people are very taken with a creative line like this, and will go along with it right there and then, just for the hell of it.

But perhaps something more direct is called for. If you are the man in the situation, then why not simply suggest a spot of divining and then intimate that your dowsing rod is all a-quiver. Whereas if you are the woman, ask him if that is a crystal in his pocket, or is he just pleased to see you?

SHAMANISM

The practice of entering into a state of radically altered consciousness and detachment from 'reality'. Until recently, this was pursued by a relatively small number of gifted individuals in ethnic, rural societies; but with the advent of Urban Shamanism, it seems that just about everyone is going around in some kind of a trance state.

SHARING

A euphemism for 'talking about oneself'. A whole distinct language has now evolved in sharing circles. Strictly correct forms of response in particular have become established, and it is vital to observe them in order to follow protocol. Examples are: "I hear what you're saying", "I really like where you're coming from", and (when the listener reaches ultimate boredom) "Thank you for sharing."

SHIATSU

A very large, very dominant type of Japanese dog, renowned for the way it is able to literally walk all over its master or mistress. The name means 'toilet training very difficult'.

SOLSTICE

Summer and Winter Solstice are simply terms for Midsummer and Christmas respectively, which make the user seem incredibly evolved, aware, sensitive, spiritually orientated and politically correct. Observing these alternatives brings the added advantages of not having to get up at the traditional crack of dawn on Midsummer's Day, and not having to get up at all on December 25th (or give anyone any presents). And best of all, nobody says things like ". . . Only 65 shopping days left till Winter Solstice."

WINTER SOLSTICE CELEBRATION

SPACE

1. Psychic arena for the processing of issues.

2. Widely used term of disapproval or rejection, as in "I need some space", "My head needs some space", "Get out of my space", and "My boyfriend needs some space — can I crash on your floor?"

SPIRIT GUIDES

A newly-evolved form of entity which is thought to have spontaneously appeared to help humankind in its current self-created predicament. Each human being has his or her own particular guide who is always 'around' but can be summoned to proximity in times of great doubt or need on matters related to spirits; for instance, when the person needs to know whether they can have a few more whiskies without going over the limit for driving, or whether the entity should just go and call a cab for them.

It isn't only people that have spirit guides — animals have them too. For instance, dogs have Spirit Guide Dogs.

SPIRITUAL PATH

Term used to refer to any of the currently popular alternatives to the more traditional methods of dealing with the imponderables of life, viz. Catholic guilt, Protestant work ethic, Buddhist suffering, Islamic self-punishment, atheistic nihilism, existentialist despair etc etc .

STRESS

An increasingly commonly-used multi-purpose term whose popularity rests on its usefulness as a means to transfer responsibility and blame for unpleasant life experiences from oneself onto outside factors in particular and the universe in general.

STUFF

One of the most useful, versatile and important terms in use today. Stuff is always 'deep', 'unresolved' or 'heavy'. And ultimately, it is invariably around the issue of one's mother. A typical usage would be: "My partner's working through rather a lot of heavy-duty *mother stuff* just at the moment."

TAOISM

An obscure religion that was inadvertently started by the cult *Winnie the Pooh* books. Followers seek to achieve enlightenment by pondering on enigmatic, inscrutable or childish riddles. The 'bible' of Taoism is the *Tao Te Ching*, by A A Milne:

> *The Tao is empty, yet never fills up;*
> *Flowing like honey, it softly wears down mountains.*
> *When the world possesses the Tao,*
> *There is always jam for tea.*

TANTRA

(Pl. noun) Literally, childish outbursts and fits of bad temper.

TANTRIC SEX

1. An ancient and sophisticated form of sexual intercourse where not very much happens. Apparently it is becoming increasingly popular again today.

2. Sex which includes many childish outbursts and fits of bad temper.

THERAPY

Generic term for a whole new approach to solving the problems of unemployment by people becoming therapists. Many human problems, indeed, have only come into existence since someone thought up a therapy to help overcome them. Recent examples include hug therapy, *pet therapy* (qv), aversion therapy, wallowing-in-misery therapy and art therapy, ie grown-up people doing childish drawings. One of the most recently developed forms of therapy is extortion therapy — probably the least

affordable of an unaffordable genre. It is said to be very good for getting in touch with one's anger.

There is one factor common to all therapists, however, which seems to survive, no matter how diverse their practices. All therapists believe that: a) their form of therapy can help any ailment, b) their form of therapy is better than any other form of therapy, and c) that most of the other therapists practising this form of therapy are charlatans.

TRAVELLER

New Age Traveller, or **Crustie**; someone whose main characteristic (ironically, from the point of view of mainstream society) is the worry that he or she might *not* move on. In point of fact, the worst thing that travellers have done is to have purloined almost exclusive media use of the term 'New Age', which used to mean something much more wide-ranging, far-reaching and profound in scope.

BAGGAGE FOR CONSCIOUS TRAVELLERS

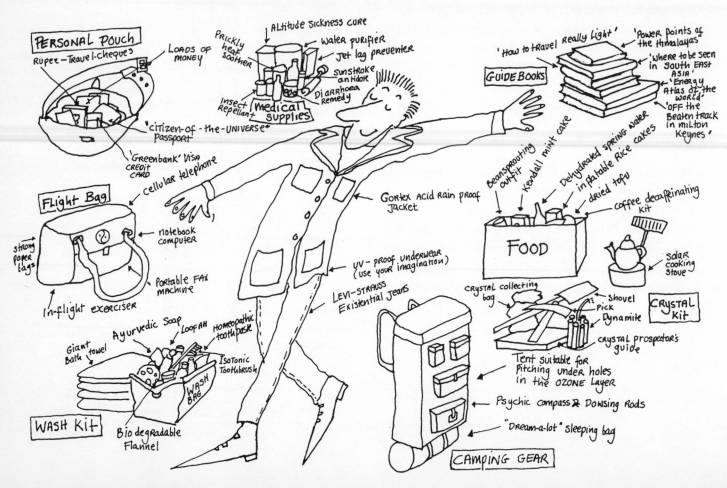

UFO SPOTTING

A more trendy, up-to-date, politically correct, slightly more interesting version of train-spotting. UFO spotters are most frequently encountered in the Crop-Circle zone of Wiltshire, the remote North of Scotland, or any pub selling organic scrumpy. UFO spotters (together with **Crop-Circle** spotters) can sometimes be identified by their purple anoraks, Birkenstock sandals worn with socks, loose-leaf notebooks, night-vision binoculars, imperfect complexion, serious demeanour and inability to be absorbed into society. The much-talked-of 'UFO belt' is a detecting device worn round the waist, especially in Wiltshire, enabling the wearer to see things other people can't.

   Like train-spotters, UFO spotters are not well understood by ordinary people; in fact they are often unjustly feared or hated, even though they are perfectly harmless. The technical term for this phenomenon is 'anorachnophobia'.

UNICORN

An animal once thought to be purely mythological, but recently shown by researchers* to have been in actuality a non-survivor of carnivorous predations aboard Noah's Ark. Their extinction is thought to have come about as a result

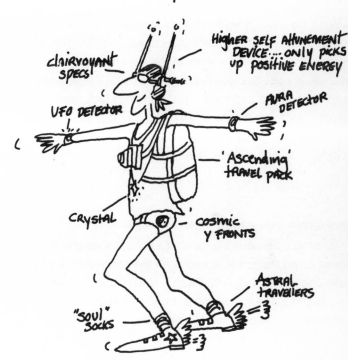

UFO spotter

- clairvoyant specs
- Higher self attunement device.... only picks up positive energy
- UFO detector
- Aura detector
- 'Ascending' travel pack
- Crystal
- cosmic y fronts
- "Soul" socks
- Astral travellers

of their extreme unpopularity among the other animals in the most popular deck game aboard the Ark — leap-frog.

* G. Larson, *Beyond the Far Side.*

VISUALISATION

Visualisation means 'seeing things', as in "Nigel is seeing things." However, the meaning has widened somewhat of late, and this is now one of the buzz-words of the 90s. Far from rejecting the 'old' values of the materialistic, possession-oriented pre-Aquarian age, with its superficial emphasis on the importance of how things look, and believing only what can be seen, the new cult of visualisation is bringing renewed credibility to looking and seeing — and then being rewarded for it.

CREATIVE VISUALISATION

This is the conscious use of positive mental visualisation to get what we want, and is based on the concept of really believing in the picture that we want to bring into reality. The subtle distinction between the Old and New approaches comes down to language. We used to talk about 'wanting something badly' but now we must 'want something well'. 'Wanting badly' reflects the negative visualisation of how rotten we will feel if we don't get what we want, whereas what we must do now is base our efforts on imagining how well we will feel when we do get it. (For other examples of Creative Childishness, see *Chanting* and *Affirmations*.)

GUIDED VISUALISATION

A guided visualisation is a very inexpensive form of holiday, where one or more people are taken on an imaginary journey by a sort of psychic Cooks tour guide. Here is a typical simple example:

"Close your eyes, and become very relaxed. Let go of all the cares and worries of the day-to-day world. Tell yourself that you are going to have a very wonderful, very beautiful, very revitalising experience.

"Now, find a very quiet place within yourself, where you know that you can always find peace and will not be disturbed. Gradually relax your whole body — from the tips of your toes right up to the end of each hair on the top of your head. You are feeling completely relaxed, totally carefree and utterly peaceful.

"Now, see yourself walking out of your house and into a very large and beautiful garden. All around you are beds of flowers, all in blossom. Ahead of you is a clear, crystal fountain, bubbling away happily. You feel your spirits lift as you see the water cascade high into the sky, and you realise that this represents the inspiration that you need. Birds are singing in the trees over your head, which have the brightest, greenest leaves you have ever seen. In the distance is a dazzling vista of verdant meadows, of deep valleys and tall mountains. You are at one with nature. The sky is clear, a deep azure blue. The sun is beaming down brightly onto the whole scene. You can feel a light breeze on your face. You feel very, very well.

"As you stroll happily around your secret garden, the birds flit alongside and small wild animals scurry round your feet.

An atmosphere of total harmony pervades the scene. You seem to be able to glide along effortlessly, never growing tired. You pass through elaborate terraces and honeysuckle-covered pergolas, into scented herb-gardens and fruit-laden orchards. All your senses seem to be heightened. Eventually you come to a very old walled garden. Here there is complete tranquillity and stillness; even the birds seem hushed in reverence to the sacredness of this place. You feel deeply at peace with yourself. You approach a rose bush. At its crown there is a single crimson rose bud. Its colour is incredibly vivid. As you look more closely, the bud begins to open, until it is in full bloom. Looking into its centre, you realise that this rose is you and, just like it, you too are starting to open up, blossoming into the wonderful potential of your true self. Stay with this feeling of unfoldment, of oneness, of inner calm, peace and radiance for a few minutes.

"Walking further on now through the walled garden, you come to a large, deep and beautiful pond, in the centre of which is a brilliant white waterlily. Sure enough, as you watch, its petals too unfold, in ring after ring of pristine brilliance. Immediately you are aware that this is the thousand-petalled lotus of your cosmic being.

"Suddenly, you have the urge to dive straight into the water of the pond — and so you do. Down, down, down you plunge; you can see easily through the water, which is crystal-clear; fish swim by, caressing your skin as you dive yet deeper still. All at once you are aware of another consciousness near you, and look round to see the friendly face of a dolphin. To your surprise, you can communicate with it just by thinking. "Hold on to my tail," it seems to say, and you do so, trusting it completely. Now you are pulled

downwards into the depths at thrilling speed; around you the water is growing darker, comforting and womb-like. You suddenly realise that you can magically breathe underwater, and you let yourself go with the motion.

"Then it is time to come up again, and the dolphin pulls you to the surface. But now you are in the shallow water at the edge of a beautiful, tropical shore, whose white sand is fringed with tall palms that sway in the gentle, cooling breeze. Drawing yourself up onto the beach in the shade of the palms, you wave goodbye to the dolphin as it speeds off to sea, leaping into the air from time to time until it is only a speck on the horizon. You lie on the beach, drinking in the exotic scents carried on the breeze. You doze in blissful torpidity. You are very, very happy. You haven't a care in the world.

"When you awake, it is to see a bright green snake looking at you from the edge of the jungle. Its eye is bright and friendly. It seems to be beckoning you. Rising, you see it indicating a path into the trees; it looks round to see that you are following. You are filled with a deep and wondrous sense of curiosity and adventure, and you follow close behind. As you pass deeper into the rainforest, the air, pleasantly cool, resounds with the rhythmic jungle insect sounds. You come upon a stream, and here the snake indicates to you that you are to follow this stream, which you realise represents the way back to your own personal inner source. The snake slides off into the jungle, its task completed.

"As you pass on, the ground begins to rise, the air becomes cooler still and the jungle sounds abate. You realise that you are now in the forest zone, where tall pines form a cathedral-like canopy. The air is imbued with an utterly peaceful yet exhilarating serenity.

"Well, quite a few things happen after that, and we'll skip some of the detail because it's pretty much standard. You keep on going up through the forest and into the zone of mists, and you keep going through that, and then you're onto the mountain proper, which you can tell because it is barren and bleak and quite cold really, but you never feel anything other than really great, because that's how these things work.

VISUALIZATION

At this point, of course, you realise that this part is all about contacting your Higher Self and so on. So next you have to find this cave that always has a fire burning outside it, and inside the cave there will be a very wise old man, or better still an old woman or crone, which is more popular these days, and of course you realise that this is your guide, so you ask them a whole string of questions about yourself, because you want to get the best value you can from the whole experience. After all, you've probably paid for it.

"Then of course it's time to go back down the mountain and back to reality, so this big eagle appears magically and you climb onto its back and are whisked away, unless of course before that you want to go in for the optional extra involving a doorway that takes you along a mysterious passage which leads into a huge underground temple where there's a ball of golden light that passes into you and down all your chakras and also this fabulous treasure that you can take away, which represents the richness of your inner wisdom or something. Or you can have the other option of following the stream down until it becomes a big river and then you see your mother across on the other side, and there's this sort of umbilical cord thing that connects your two navels — yes, right across the river — and you have to say nice things to your mother and then you get out your Swiss Army camping knife and cut this cord which then falls off both of you into the river and is washed down to the sea and is presumably eaten by fish. Or the dolphin. But you don't have to bother with the pond bit on the way back, it's pretty boring the second time around, so you can skip that out and come straight back. So then you wake up again, back in the drug rehabilitation centre, feeling much better; feeling refreshed, relaxed, revitalised and really, really good."

WATER

At one time, water was a clear, odourless, tasteless, drinkable fluid which was, in fact, supplied to each home in the land, and which people could actually avail themselves of by the simple expedient of rotating a device known as a 'tap' in an anti-clockwise direction, and safely drink. Furthermore, it was actually free. In recent years, however, that original product has been withdrawn and replaced by a more saleable commodity known as:

MINERAL WATER

Mineral water, in turn, once was simply water with some minerals in it, but this too has changed; in the interests of further increased saleability, it has been replaced by a product that doesn't have any minerals — such as salts — and today usually boasts the fact. So-called mineral water, then, has become a clear, odourless, tasteless, drinkable fluid, like 'water' used to be.

However, there is a lot more to the matter than that. Drinking mineral water has evolved into an art-form in itself, requiring knowledge, skill, discrimination, a strong sense of fashion and rather a lot of money.

Even ten years ago, no one could have suspected the possibilities latent in this product. Below is just a selection of some prominent brands that have established themselves in this hugely competitive field. France, of course got in there first and still dominates the upper end of the market — the 'Hautes Wateurs', as they are fond of calling them — but steady inroads are constantly being made by new labels from sources as diverse as Bulgaria, Chile, Mozambique, Tibet and Wagga Wagga in New South Wales.

Eaujolais Nouveau

Literally, 'very nice new water'. Every April in the rainy season, supplies are bottled and rushed across country by oxcart from the wadis in French Guinea, to be greeted by eager English buyers who meet the hydrofoil from Calais and drink the water amidst wild celebrations on the cliffs of Dover. Usually arrives on or around October 31st.

Côte de Mediocrité

An impudent upstart of an Eau de Table from the terraces of Anodin, France, this water has pretensions far beyond its station; arrogantly condescending, it taunts the palette with empty promises.

Chateau Neuf du Pipe

One of the very great waters, this Grand Cru Methode Champagnoise is the zenith of the master craftsman's art. Complex and profound, it is laden with quince and blackberries and notes of almond and pepper; it is aromatic with fennel, redolent of truffles and foies gras, and oh! such a bouquet of honeysuckle. Full-bodied, sensuous, heavy with innuendo, it speaks of seductive intent; replete with velvet desire, it proffers delicate kisses and undercurrents of virile muscularity. Long after its passionate currents have run their heady course, subtle aftertastes eddy and swirl on the palate, lapping for ever, it seems, on the mouth's shores. Beware imitations.

Dippe de Mouton

This rather abrasive Eau de Pays from Cadenet is probably best avoided by those with a sensitive palette, or an allergic reaction to animal fur. Thinned down with retsina, though, expatriot Englanders in Provence find it makes an excellent stripping agent for pine furniture.

Ijsberg 1912

An incredibly rare vintage which is impossible to obtain on the open market since the very limited supply only became available in 1990 upon the raising of the Titanic, and was immediately snapped up by collectors. Originally bottled specially for the ship's maiden voyage, only three crates were recovered from its hold. Legend has it that an obsession with serving this water adequately chilled on that journey had much to do with the tragedy that ensued.

Appellation Spring

Something of a redneck among more classy waters, this label from the mountains of the Eastern USA has bright musical notes, but is marred by an excessive number of fiddly bits. It is nonetheless making a name for itself, going down especially well at hoedowns, barndances and bar-room brawls.

Lancashire Spa

A dark, smoky North English water. Heavy with earthy flavours, it fills the palette with sulphur and brickdust, and heaps of slag and coalshale. A meal in itself really, although southern connoisseurs may have difficulty with its gritty textures.

Nature's Brook, 100% Organic

This quintessentially English water, with its strong presence of courgettes and compost, may also be a bit hard for some to take, but it's quite the thing to be seen drinking at a Green Party conference, hunt-sab ball or free-range hen-party!

Limey Gutbuster

A robust, highly alkaline brew from the Australian outback, produced strictly for export. First brought over to Britain in the luggage of the victorious touring cricket side of 1989, it has a highly roasted flavour, burnt overtones and a strong, sour aftertaste of ashes. Cricket fans, of course, wouldn't give a XXXX for anything else.

Ballyslipper

The archetypal Irish water; thick with stout, broguish accents and more than a touch of the Blarney, it compares favourably with its somewhat more Presbyterian Scottish counterpart, **Sporran Bru**. The latter, though, is a far more subdued water, almost too quiet for many drinkers, bottled as it has been since mediaeval times by the non-speaking Tappiste monks at Findhorn Abbey.

Reservoire Speciale du Camellfort 1988

The unique qualities of this exceptional West-of-England water stem from the addition of a unique blend of hand-chosen ingredients, one of the most closely guarded secrets in the business, known only to one or two operatives at the bottlers, Cornwall Water Authority.

Aqua Scorpio

Latest of the immensely successful range of astrological fizzies. This one has a bit of a sting in its tail.

All in all, then, an extremely varied selection. But what does the future hold in store in this high-pressure millrace of a market? Experts certainly agree that products from exotic sources are going to grow at the expense of the more mundane or established brands. French producers in particular will continue to lose their grip in such a slippery commercial environment, especially if they persist in their elitist attitudes. Indeed, due to gross overproduction, they already have some embarrassing water lakes over there.

But make no mistake — the habit of drinking water is percolating steadily into all strata of society, filtering through to the ordinary person in the street by an inexorable process of osmosis. Former giants of the industry — notably the now stagnant Poirier — have failed to recognise this at their cost . Of course, there is always room at the upper end for the genuinely superior product,and there will always be a demand for the elite and collectable waters among those who are laying down a noteworthy cellar. In this category, look out especially for the Pineaus and Meauselles and, for more serious drinkers, the Graves.

Looking to potential newcomers on the international scene, we will definitely see classy contributions from California, where study of French results is beginning to bear fruit; also from Russia, whose massive pre-war vintage water cellars are only now being unearthed following the dismemberment of the USSR and its regime.

The Japanese, as usual, are going one better than all the rest. Coming straight into the market-place, one step ahead of the competition, they are about to unveil the result of years of government-sponsored research into aquatic genetic engineering. Any moment now, they will launch their solution to the biggest problem inherent in mineral water production, storage and shipping — ie its sheer bulk and weight. Japan's answer? Dehydrated water.

WICCA

The stuff that witches' baskets are made from.

WORKSHOPS

A workshop is exactly like a class or course except that it is more expensive and is on a more bizarre or esoteric topic, such as 'Transcendental Vegetation', 'Build Your Own Computer from Recycled Lentils' or 'The Willie as a Healing Tool'.

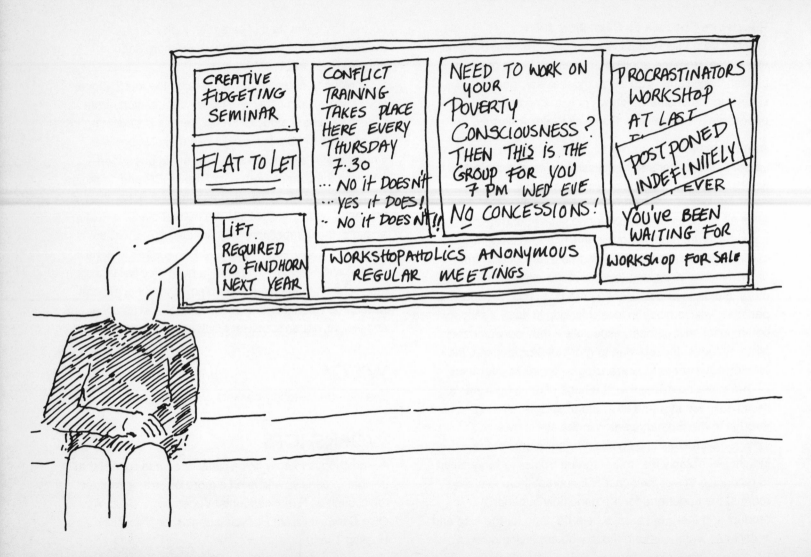

YIN AND YANG

A highly pervasive oriental concept, which seeks to explain how Life, the Universe and Everything works by saying that there are only two different kinds of thing, and that everything everywhere is either one or the other. However, the concept is now completely discredited, since it has been realised that dividing things into only two categories in an either/or format is discriminatory, divisive, elitist, politically incorrect and not at all cool any more.

This was, in fact, well known to our ancient occidental forefathers, such as the Celts, who realised that every important philosophical statement about the nature of reality should involve subdivisions into not two but three. However, this all got lost in the mists of time. Yin and Yang even caught on in a big way in recent times in the West. In fact, the latent existential shortcomings of Yin and Yang have been completely ignored until the re-publication in 1993 of Karl Popper's long out-of-print classic *Yin, Yang and Jung*.

YOGHURT

A traditional form of cultured food, once belonging purely in the realm of the alternative food buff, but which in recent decades has become all the rage in the mainstream. Thus it is no longer found palatable by serious, aware, discriminating faddists. There is now an extraordinary variety of forms of yoghurt; some of the most popular include sheepsmilk yoghurt, goatsmilk yoghurt, soymilk yoghurt, plain yoghurt, fruit yoghurt, low-fat yoghurt, rich creamy yoghurt, natural yoghurt, live yoghurt, dead yoghurt, Hatha yoghurt, Iyengar yoghurt and Karma yoghurt.

ZEN

A once-significant term whose content of meaning has systematically become diminished through persistent over-use, until today it means nothing at all, as in 'Zen in the Art of Archery', 'Zen in the Art of Motorcycle Maintenance', 'Zen in the Art of Making a Nice Cup of Tea' etc etc.

ZEN TEABAGS

Generic term for particularly 'cute' words or phrases that are thought up on the spur of the moment by writers needing a title for a book and other disreputable individuals. Such phrases have absolutely no meaning, but are passed off as authentic expressions which the listener or reader is supposed to feel embarrassed about not knowing the meaning of. They can and do, however, fool wide audiences and often take on purely random meanings, ultimately passing into common parlance, eg 'archetype', 'semiotic' or 'New Man'.

Oscar Wilde is widely regarded as the patron saint of Zen Teabaggism.

ZORROASTRIANISM

An ancient and far-fetched system of religion, whose object of worship was a black-clad masked figure, who (its followers claimed) would reappear thousands of years later, around 1950 AD in fact, on something called television. Zorroastrianism has thus left its mark (sic) on a whole generation of western TV watchers, most of whom, however, are now dead.

Advertisement

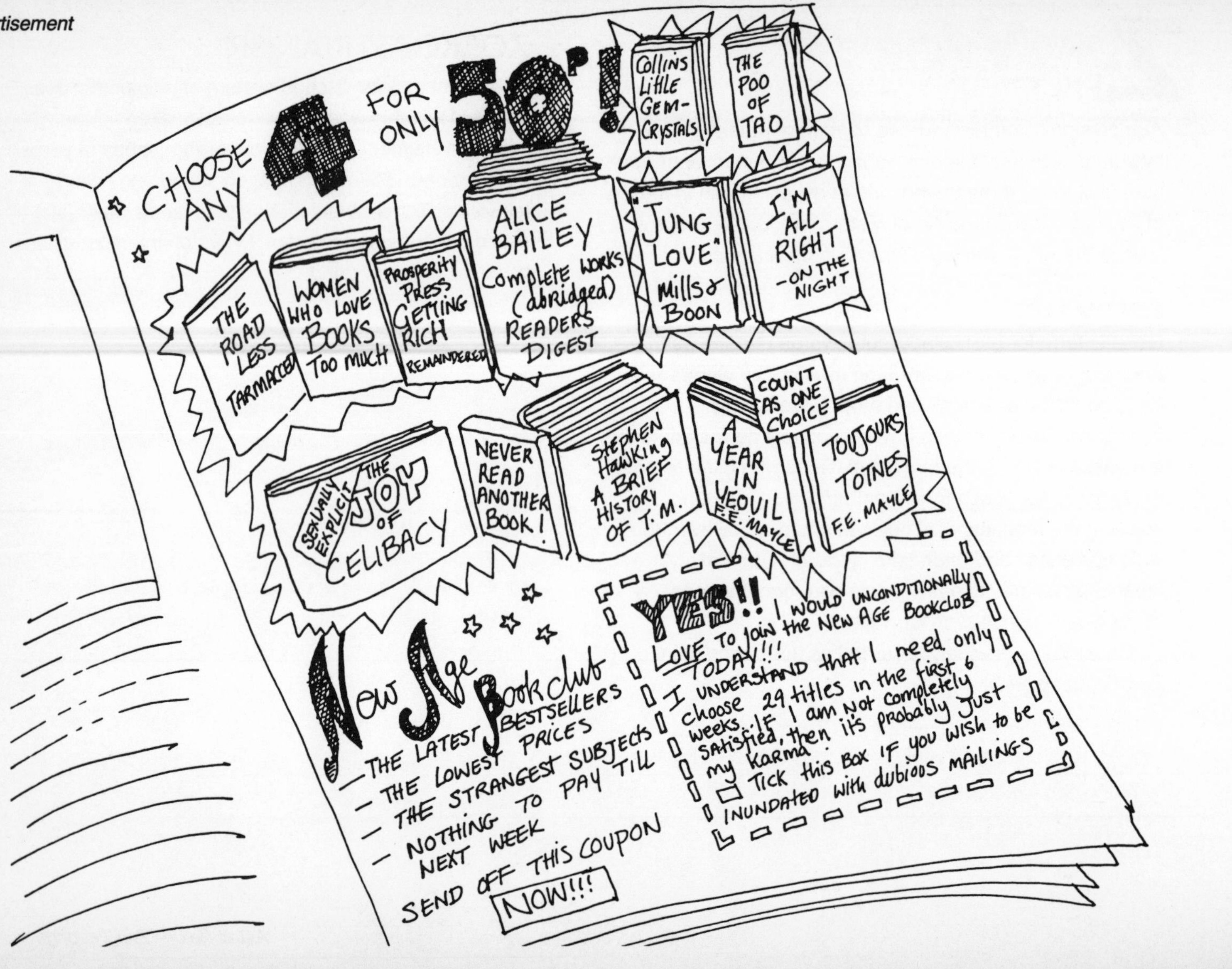

NEW WORDS

The following words have become a part of New Age parlance in very recent times, and are not widely known even in specialist circles. Judicious use of these terms will mark the user out as one at the cutting edge of semantic progress, evolutionary awareness and general enlightenment.

ĂM´WAY LADY *(n.)*

A person of either sex who tends to lose all their friends through trying to build them into elaborate structures for pyramid selling.

ĂSS´PAINS *(pl. n.)*

Irritating individuals who, when you inform them that you have broken your leg, have had your home broken into, or have lost a close friend or relative, enquire what you must have done to 'manifest this', or what it must be 'trying to teach you'.

ĂTLĂ´NT *(n.)*

Any individual who can give you a detailed run-down on every past life they have ever had, but who is quite incapable of managing or even thinking about everyday affairs in their current manifestation.

BEA´VERWEAVER *(n.)*

A male who poses as a shaman, purely in order to pull women.

BĔ´NDERSPAWN *(n.)*

Small children belonging to **New Age Travellers**.

BREE´ZEBĀBIES *(pl. n.)*

Those people who think that there is no major life problem, or neurosis or handicap that cannot be suddenly and permanently transformed and healed overnight. They are usually the offspring — or parents — of **stuckbirthers** (qv).

BŬ´ZZFLY *(n.)*

Someone who constantly flits from one Personal Transformation course to the next. Differs from the **scantling** (qv) in that he or she is purely a consumer rather than purveyor.

CĂ´TBĂGGER (n.)

An inexperienced and unqualified therapist who consistently opens clients' most traumatic cans of worms, and then leaves them to deal with the consequences on their own.

FĬ´XĬTER (n.)

Someone who, upon meeting new people socially at dinner parties, on picnics or at private art views, insists on providing them with unsolicited astrological guidance, clairvoyant readings or foreboding holistic health diagnoses.

GU´RUNŎTS (pl. n.)

Beings who claim to be Totally Enlightened Masters, when they are in fact only workshop leaders with expensive PR. Everyone knows that the last thing a truly Enlightened Master needs or wants to do is to tell everyone this fact. Soft-focus lens shots on publicity material and a studio light placed behind the head are dead giveaways.

Ĭ´SSŪESMĬTH (n.)

The type of person who is always *about* to deal with all their unresolved stuff, and go forward with their plans for life, *just* as soon as they have moved out of their current house/ got out of their current destructive relationship/ brought up their current children.

PEA´CEMONGERS (aka BĬ´tterlĬngs) (pl. n.)

People who always end their letters with expressions such as 'Blessings, love and light', when they are actually seething with internal rage, malice and hate.

PĔSSŎ´PTĬMĬSM (n.)

An increasingly common human ailment. When you meet someone with this condition, they will tell you that they have *just* come out of a very bad patch, but that things are really great now. Then when you meet them a year later, they say that things were very difficult *last year*, but they really feel on course *now*. If you meet them the following month, they tell you how awful it has been for the past four weeks or so, but that things are really *fantastic* now. And so on.

PŎ´DGERS (pl. n.)

Well-meaning individuals who present themselves as healers, but are clearly unable to sort even themselves out. *Even* themselves? *Especially* themselves!

POU´NDPĬNCHERS (pl. n.)

People who offer very expensive workshops on 'Overcoming Poverty Consciousness'.

PŬ´TTYBŬNNY (n.)

A heroic individual who fanatically pursues the path of personal transformation, becoming totally obsessed with the process of change itself, as in: "Yes, I'm doing really well. I've changed so much in the past X weeks/ months/ years/ decades." This can so annoy one's partner/ family/ employer that they may pretend they don't recognise one any more, so that one may be obliged to find a new home, job and complete set of friends.

SCA´NTLĬNG (n.)

An eclectic healer who has learned about twenty-nine different therapies at weekend workshops, and is not afraid to use them. Also **SCA´NTLETTE** — a person who sets up in practice in a therapy after studying it for a couple of minutes while browsing in a bookshop.

SCHLŬMP (n.)

This is a particular mood — a kind of quiet, serious, humourless and emotionally suppressed intensity, which in some circles is regarded as the proper attitude for spiritually-oriented or ecologically-aware people to assume at all times.

SCRŬNT (n.)

Person who never seems to have any money, but is always complaining about those who 'sell out', work for a living and *do* have money. Collective term: a 'whinge' of scrunts.

SPŪR´IŌS (pl. n.)

'Unsolicited' testimonials used to advertise products or services, to verify how amazing they are. Key features are random capitalised phrases, lots of superlatives, and the inappropriateness of blatant materialism to the kind of product being advertised, eg ". . . I found your Instant Enlightenment Intensives INCREDIBLY POWERFUL . . . they are TOTALLY AMAZING. I now have TOTAL CONTROL over EVERY ASPECT of my own life . . . stepping beyond my FEARS . . . eliminating BLOCKAGES . . . words cannot describe . . . etc etc."

STŬ´CKBÎRTHER (n.)

One who believes that, no matter what lengths you go to, you will never, ever be able to properly heal or fully recover from the profound traumas and hurts of the past. The opposite of a *breezebaby*.

TĀ´OSER (n.)

Perpetual seeker after truth who spends a whole lifetime searching out, converting to, and then giving up one spiritual path after another.

TŎ´TNEY *(n.)*

Anyone who has spoken exclusively in New Age jargon since birth.

VĀ´GUEY *(n.)*

A person who is unable to take the slightest step, or make even the smallest personal decision, without first consulting an oracle, or seeing a psychic or preferably undergoing a lengthy course in therapy.

VĔ´NTURE-HEAD *(n.)*

An entrepreneur who sets up one New-Age-type business after another, none of which ever seems to succeed.

XĔ´NORĀTE *(v.)*

To pretend that some artefact, process or custom is authentically Native American, ancient Tibetan or of extra-terrestrial origin, in order to enhance its attractiveness and perceived worth, so as to sell it at a higher price or gain kudos from having it on your coffee-table (which will, of course, be de-caffeinated).

Appendix 1:

Future History of the New Age

as transcribed from the Akashic Records (qv)

1998: The first hint of serious impending change — a British politician admits that he was wrong about something. The Opposition party is flummoxed.

1999: Radical change sets in for good. The Tory government brings in an amended national curriculum for schools. Maths, science and English are out; meditation, divination, seeing auras and healing by numbers are in.

2020: Precocious school leavers from the 1990s begin to exert a dominant influence on society. There is a total ban on television violence, soap operas and British sitcoms. Life insurance can only be obtained by non-smoking, psychic vegans.

2040: Ecological awareness and new voting patterns bring changes in leadership around the world. Even the British Conservatives cannot change policy often enough to survive. Norway declares the oceans of the world an international whale park. A dolphin becomes prime minister of Japan. Manhattan is returned to the Native Americans. Antarctica is handed back to the penguins, in exchange for a bucketful of herrings.

2055: Cure found for the common cold. Fossil fuels run out. Corn circles mystery solved. Hamburgers become extinct. Stonehenge found to be a hoax. The bit of paper with the formula for making plastic written on it is lost. Indigenous pine forest, spreading out from the Scottish Highlands, engulfs London. UFOs re-designated 'FOs'. Parents stop making statements like, "Things were never like this in *our* day", and "Why don't you listen to some *proper* music?"

2070: Society has now totally polarised into two groups — those who are attached to materialism, authoritarianism and the old values, and those who are in natural harmony with the incoming era of love, light and spiritual development.

2071: A cataclysmic global series of earthquakes, tidal waves and natural disasters, emanating from California, swallows up all the people who were attached to materialism, authoritarianism and the old values, together with dentists who wouldn't see people on the National Health.

2072: Following these dramatic global events, and totally unpredicted by any astrologers anywhere, the Earth's axis spontaneously shifts by 23 degrees from magnetic north. The third Ice Age immediately begins, exactly offsetting the damaging effects of the previously prevailing Greenhouse syndrome, and thus producing what comes to be known as the 'Greengage Effect', because soft fruit can now be grown outdoors anywhere on the planet.

2100: Further change to agricultural patterns has set in. Biodynamic cultivation has now evolved to the point where vegetables are grown in the air. Corresponding human physiological change has also taken place. Cooking is no longer necessary: humans now possess a three-stomach ruminant digestive system, allowing processing of high-chlorophyll grass-like plants. Soon after this, the human gizzard evolves, and people remember how to fly. Men can become pregnant; but very few want to.

2215: Crime, illness and religion are now obsolete. A large group of extra-terrestrials who have been occupying human forms in Sedona, Arizona since the 1970s decide that the Earth is now ready for their teachings. They spread over the planet, offering adult education classes in High Evolution subjects. Radical economic and political change permeates all continents. Greed becomes extinct; the emphasis is now on economic shrinkage rather than growth. 'Nuclear peace' breaks out all over the planet.

Efforts are now towards giving up land rather than gaining it. Saddam Hussein is awarded the posthumous Nobel Peace Prize. The Troubles end in Northern Ireland. In Glasgow, Rangers invite Celtic over for tea. Milton Keynes wins the World Cup. Ordinary people organise raffles in order to get rid of their personal property; estate agents, who shrewdly escaped the Cataclysm, continue to earn fees through helping them find takers. Everyone is extremely happy and contented.

2313: Politics and money are now obsolete. Spiritual enlightenment becomes available in a small blue package inside potato crisp packets, even though food is now also obsolete.

2370: Speech is superseded as a means of communication — thought transfer is used instead. People only talk to each other as a kind of entertaining rhetorical device, e.g. if you want to pretend that you are angry (in much the same way, curiously, that the primitive peoples in the 20th century would use silence to the same effect).

2500: The power of thought is extended to cover physical movement — you just wish to be somewhere else and you are immediately there. Travel agents, however, still manage to make a living, because: a) some clients still need guidance on the 'in' places to transmogrify to, and b) they are even more tenacious than estate agents. Lunar honeymoons and a really good tan from summer on Mars are all the rage, but a lot of people still want to get back home in time for tea.

2550: Shangri-la is found. It was just off the M1 near the Watford Gap all along. The secret of immortality is discovered; but it doesn't really catch on. Nobody needs it any more.

2600: Problems are now officially obsolete. Almost everything is officially obsolete. The police are re-invented as a purely recreational measure. Their function is to encourage imaginative and creative misbehaviour, among people who feel that their lives lack depth. Hospitals re-open, to accommodate those whose health is unbearably perfect, and prisons are reinstated, for those whom everyone hates because they are just too *nice*.

2999: Despite these desperate measures, endemic boredom breaks out all over the planetary village, and no real cure can be found. However, a secret, fanatically religious underground group has formed, who warn that a great cataclysmic disaster is approaching, which will engulf all those who do not give up attachment to universal love, light, spiritual development and the old values, and join together in natural harmony with the new era of materialism, authoritarianism and general Endarkenment . . .

APPENDIX 2:

QUESTIONNAIRE

How 'New Age' are You?

Here is a chance to discover your 'NAQ' — your New Age Quotient. After reading the book, you can test your grasp of the concepts. But remember, it isn't about being 'better' or 'worse', or about getting a high score. For each question just tick the answer that seems most right for you. Be spontaneous, rather than getting too anguished about it. Then add up your 'score' using the codes provided and check the interpretation given at the end.

1. You are a vegetarian. Dining at the home of your partner's parents, you are served a dish of sheep's eye-balls. Do you:

a. Gobble them up and ask for more?
b. Pretend to eat, but hide them in your pocket?
c. Make polite conversation about the ozone layer?
d. Call off the whole relationship with your partner?

2. Which of these categories of people annoys you the most?

a. People who are forever saying, "I had an intuition this was going to happen"?

b. People who are always wishing something different was happening from what *is* happening?

c. People like yourself?

d. Everyone?

3. You are an atheist, and your wife is a hard-line Catholic, but your teenage son suddenly declares a wish to convert to Sufism. Do you:

a .Buy him a copy of *The Tao of Pooh*?

b. Give him a one-way ticket to Istanbul?

c. Arrange a bar mitzvah immediately?

d. Make a nice cup of tea?

4. Which of the following best describes your sex life:

a. AC/DC?
b. Battery/mains?
c. Never/occasionally/sometimes/often/all the time?
d. What sex life?

5. You go to a party and see some friends of yours, who you know to be police, smoking a joint. Do you:

a. Give them a piece of your mind?
b. Write to your MP about it?
c. Shop them?
d. Join them for a quick spliff?

6. Which of the following 'New Age' workshops appeals most to you?

a. Knitting patterns from Atlantis?
b. 'Yin, yang and Jung'?
c. 'Personal transformation addiction and how to cure it'?
d. A long lie-in in bed all weekend?

7. You are a mother and your child asks you, "Mummy, what's an orgasm?" Do you say:

a. "Don't you mean organism, dear?"
b. "Let's get a book about it from the library"?
c. "I'll tell you when you're older"?
d. "I don't know. Ask your father"?

8. You break wind audibly when friends have come round for dinner. Do you:

a. Laugh it off?
b. Blame it on the dog?
c. Explain that it's an old Eastern way of showing appreciation for food, and suggest that everyone else does the same?
d. Go red in the cheeks, and never invite those friends again?

9. Which of the following pick-up lines is most 'you'?

a. "It seems that fate is inexorably drawing us irresistibly together"?
b. "How long are you going to go on ignoring me?"
c. "Would you like to have sex with me?"
d. "How about a nice cup of tea?"

10. What do think of questionnaires?

a. I never do them.
b. I never even think of doing them.
c. I wouldn't be seen dead doing one.
d. Don't know.

INTERPRETING YOUR SCORE:

Just read off the points according to this key for each answer that you have ticked, add them up and read your interpretation below.

1. — a: 1 point; b: 3 points; c: 2 points; d: 4 points
2. — a: 2   b: 3   c: 1   d: 17
3. — a: 2   b: 3   c: 4   d: 1
4. — a: 4   b: 3   c: 2   d: 1
5. — a: 3   b: 1   c: 4   d: 2
6. — a: 1   b: 2   c: 3   d: 4
7. — a: 3   b: 1   c: 2   d: 4
8. — a: 3   b: 4   c: 2   d: 1
9. — a: 2   b: 4   c: 3   d: 1
10. — a: 2   b: 3   c: 4   d: 1

Up to 15 points:
Let's face it — you are a wimp. You've been planning to go into therapy for indecisiveness for longer than you can remember, but still haven't done it. You read your fortune in the stars every day — *and* it all seems to come true. You use low-salt salt. Oh, and you may be addicted to tea as well. Still, nobody's perfect. Try eating a bit more meat. Preferably *live* meat.

16-25 points:
You're a really enlightened being. You recycle your bottles, cans, newspapers, clothes, vegetable waste, dustbin liners, bathwater, telephone directories and the trimmings from your haircuts. You have just stopped voting Green because it's too conventional. You fast once a week on organic kiwi-fruit. Congratulations! But have you any friends?

26-35 points:
You aren't fooling anyone but yourself — you seem to be very right-on, way-out and laid-back, but deep down inside you are a very superficial person. You need to go to a workshop, or *something*.

Over 35 points:
You are not a nice person. You always expect other people to come around to your way of thinking, and you never meet anyone half-way. You are unable to suppress your anger, bitterness, frustration or resentment. You believe passionately in the expediency of creative greed and self-centredness. You probably stole this book just to do this questionnaire, in order to feel better about yourself. No doubt you cheated with the answers. You'll do very well in the New Age. Probably in real life too.

CKNOWLEDGEMENTS

Anyone who really hates this book should also resent the following people, who were instrumental and supportive in its forthcoming:

My agent, Susan Mears.

Sandra Kramer and Karin Bogliolo at Findhorn Press; Alan Harfield and others at Posthouse Printing & Publishing.

These individuals, who provided verbal inspiration or practical support: Yannis Androcopoulos, Hugh Stevens, Sue Townsend, Nigel Berman, Fil, Maureen at Colourfast Photocopying, Dulcie Domum, Toine Rongen, Sue Limb, Geoffrey Ellis, Jude Payne and Ruth Sheldrick of WIRE design studio.

Mr Cairns, my teacher at Rosetta Primary School, Belfast.

Elaine Bellamy, who sometimes let me off washing the dishes so that I could write the book.

. . . and my Dad and Mum.

I am grateful to them all.

GT

The illustration team at work . . .

ANNE WARD

Anne Ward is a cartoonist and illustrator who specialises in soft, New Age targets. She is eminently qualified for this by having brought up three children in the bitterly feudal society of idealistic communities, and by currently living in Totnes.

Anne has illustrated a number of books, including *Out of Your Head — The Only Place to Be* by Eddie and Debbie Shapiro, and *Change For the Better* by Patricia Davis. She is currently working on several other book projects.

Anne and Gerry have collaborated for several years on cartoon production, for a wide variety of straight and unstraight magazines and newspapers, and for *The Whole Person Catalogue* by Mike Considine. They are still talking to each other.

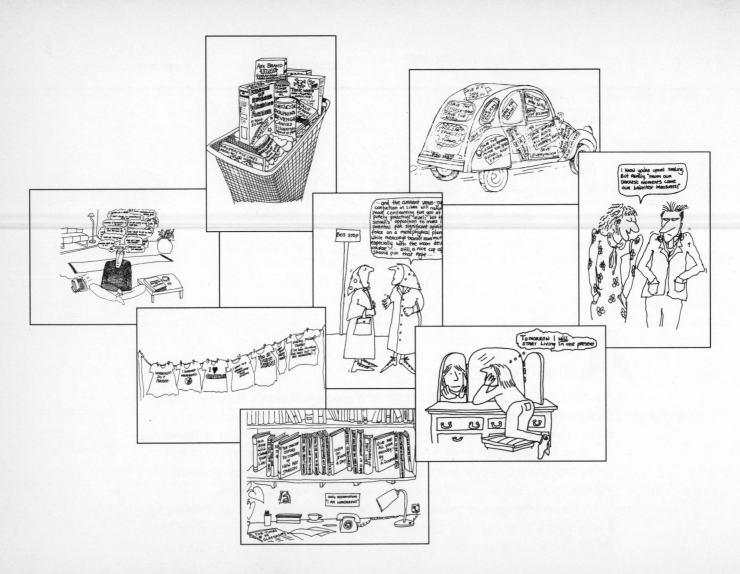

POSTCARDS

Some of the cartoons in this book, as shown on facing page, are available as postcards in packs of 8 assorted cards.

Price: £2.00 per pack (including packing & postage to anywhere in the world)

Please complete and detach the order form opposite, or write your order on a separate piece of paper. Enclose payment and send to:

**Phoenix by Mail,
The Park,
Findhorn,
Forres IV36 0TZ,
Scotland.**

(Tel. 01309 691074, Fax 01309 690933)

Please send me _____ pack(s) of *Astral Sex — Zen Teabags* postcards @ £2.00 each (postage and packing included)

Total amount enclosed = £_____

Name _____

Address _____

_____

_____

Visa/Access/Mastercard accepted.

Card no. _____

Expiry date _____

Signature _____